636800

D1085484

Live Until
You Die

Live Until
You Die

RANDOLPH CRUMP MILLER

A PILGRIM PRESS BOOK

from
United Church Press
Philadelphia

Library of Congress Cataloging in Publication Data

Miller, Randolph Crump, 1910-
  Live until you die.
  "A Pilgrim Press book."
  Includes bibliographical references.
  1. Death. I. Title.
BT825.M5   236'.1   73-8657
ISBN 0-8298-0253-3

Acknowledgments for the use of copyrighted materials are
given in the Preface and in footnotes.

United Church Press, 1505 Race Street,
Philadelphia, Pennsylvania 19102

**To our posterity,
our grandchildren**

Danielle Collette Symonds
David Christopher Symonds
Deborah Christine Symonds
Dudley Vaughan Fowlkes
Paschal Dupuy Fowlkes
Christopher Laurance Rand
Elizabeth Randolph Rand
James Edward Leahy, Jr.
Elizabeth Vaughan Carroll

Contents

Preface

This is a book about living meaningfully until we die. In it we look at the process of dying and the fact of death. You and I are going to die; there is no escape. How can we live so that we confront our dying in a wholesome frame of mind?

In recent years there has been some research into the process of dying, so that we have a good deal of psychological, sociological, and medical information. Involved in these studies have been doctors, psychologists, sociologists, and clergymen, especially chaplains in hospitals and those involved in the clinical training of ministerial students. These findings are invaluable for our purpose.

Because the natural man faces death no matter what his religious outlook is, I have paid less attention to the various religious interpretations in the earlier chapters, saving this kind of thinking for the final three chapters where we ask about the meaning of living and dying in today's world. The need first is to understand the empirical evidence about how we die, and this information is helpful as a basis for developing our attitude toward it.

We need to look at the way dying and death are interpreted in our culture, at the psychological fear of death, at how children come to an understanding of death, at our denial and acceptance of death with the ambiguity that this implies, at a realistic view of death from an ethical perspective, at the experiences and attitudes of those who know death is approaching, at how to die with dignity, including planning for our own death and funeral. Then we can turn to what the Bible says, look at the meaning of hope in this life and hereafter, and finally understand what it means to live life at the limit.

If this is not enough, there is a suggested list of books at the end.

Jürgen Moltmann makes clear the need for the art of dying when he writes that

an ethic of accepted, loved, and experienced life must, for its part, practice attitudes toward death and liberate dying from its repression or glamorization. As life and love are an art, the ability to die is also an art. We indeed know, in the double sense, how one can "take life" but we know very little about how one can leave it humanly and with dignity. Man has a right to his own death in the same way as he has a right to his life.[1]

For this, there is a need for death education, and this book seeks to provide it in a simple and straightforward way.

The book was suggested by one of the editors of United Church Press, possibly because of a chapter on death in my *Living with Anxiety* (Pilgrim Press, 1971). I was supplied with books and suggestions as the outline and manuscript developed. My wife, with her piercing questions, has attempted to keep me "honest," so that I do not make claims that cannot be substantiated, although the reader must make a judgment on this. The Rev. Edward Dobihal, a hospital chaplain and colleague at Yale Divinity School who is the moving force behind the New Haven Hospice, has also helped me avoid inaccuracies. Another friend, Miss

---

[1] Jürgen Moltmann, *Hope and the Future of Man*, ed. Ewert H. Cousins (Philadelphia: Fortress Press, 1972), p. 104. Used by permission.

Dorothy Freeman, has checked me on the clarity of what I am trying to say.

I am grateful to the authors and publishers who have given me permission to quote copyrighted material, as indicated in the footnotes. I have used the following translations of the Bible, with these abbreviations:

G   *The Complete Bible: An American Translation* by Edgar J. Goodspeed and J. M. Powis Smith. Copyright 1939 by the University of Chicago Press.

NEB   *The New English Bible.* Copyright by the Delegates of the Oxford University Press and the Syndics of the Cambridge University Press, 1961, 1970.

PB   *The Book of Common Prayer*

RSV   *Revised Standard Version of the Bible.* Copyright 1946, 1952 by the Division of Christian Education, National Council of Churches.

TEV   *Today's English Version: The Psalms for Modern Man.* Copyright 1970 by the American Bible Society.

Randolph Crump Miller

The Divinity School
Yale University

CHAPTER ONE

Death in Our Culture

He was talking about his father's death. His father had lived to be ninety-two, which is a mighty long time. His friends consoled him, for they knew that he loved his father. But they had the idea that maybe it was not so hard on him because his father was ninety-two. It may be easier to lose a father at an advanced age. And he writes:

Certainly I was grateful for such comments. But I found myself perturbed too. Didn't they realize that to die is to die, whether you are seventeen, forty-nine, or one hundred and ten? Didn't they know that our death is our death? And that each one of us has only one death to die? This was my father's death! It was no less significant because he was most of a hundred. It was his death. The only one he would ever have.[1]

I have meditated over that comment by Joseph Mathews because it gets at the heart of this book. The art of dying may take a lifetime to learn, and all that we have learned about life helps us to learn how to die, but it all adds up to what happened to Joe's father. "It was his death. The only one he would ever have." So it is with us. We have one

---

[1] Joseph W. Mathews, "The Time My Father Died," *The Modern Vision of Death,* ed. Nathan A. Scott, Jr. (Richmond: John Knox Press, 1967), pp. 107–8. Used by permission.

death to die. It is our death. It is the only one we will ever have.

You are going to die. This is a simple, empirical fact that no one can escape. Psychologically you can deny it, repress it, or fear it; you may welcome it with psychotic overtones, or you may accept it gracefully as the end of a process of becoming and perishing, which is the essence of life. You may prefer to ignore it completely and refuse to read this book. You may be so compulsively aware of it that you read everything on the topic. But perhaps you want to become sufficiently acquainted with the subject of death that you can live creatively without worrying too much about it.

There is an art of dying which is worth careful study, for dying is part of the process of living. There is something we can identify as death education, for we cannot live fully until we have come to terms with our own dying and death. Yet, while we may have observed the death of others, there is no way in which we can experience our own death. We have difficulty imagining a condition in which we will not be. We can picture the grief of others when we are dead, but because death is the end we have no way of tying it in with any experience we have had.

We may have a rational view of death. It comes at the end of an unspecified number of years as a process of nature, and there is no escape from it. Everyone knows this with the top of his mind; but this does not account for what goes on in the depths of one's person. There is an unwitting element in the way we face living or dying that is related to our feelings, to the way we sense reality, to our imaginative and fantasy functions, and to our relationships with others. This leads many to deny the fact of death, as many primitive people have done. We have inherited many emotional responses which are precritical, and some of these result in being attracted to alternatives to the conclusion that death is final. It is this unwitting factor that competes with clear thinking about death, and if we are to be capable of the "art of dying" we need to discover how to overcome these deep-seated and often less than rational attitudes toward death.

Many years ago Sir Thomas Browne wrote: "The long habit of living indisposeth me for dying."[2] This is a healthy attitude, for it stresses the importance of focusing on life and placing thoughts about death in the background. But unless we have come to terms with dying and death, at least to a degree, we do not live fully. Our thoughts about death, when buried in escape mechanisms, have a way of over-powering us at moments when we should be seeing the meaning of life. We may agree with Spinoza, who wrote that "a free man thinks of nothing less than of death, and his wisdom is not a meditation upon death but upon a life."[3] This could be a symptom of Spinoza's healthy-mindedness in that he was "not led by the fear of death," for he had come to terms with a subject hardly worth mentioning; or it could have been an avoidance of a subject about which little can be said.

In the Bible death is first mentioned in connection with human beings to show that their days are numbered, as are those of animals. But for human beings death is an evil to be postponed, an enemy, partly because it is the end and partly because it is not the end, for even in the Jewish Bible there is an emphasis on a life continuing in the place of the departed where one is separated from God. There are inti-mations of immortality in some of the later books and these carry over into the New Testament, along with belief in resurrection. But death as a fact remains as an end of this life, no matter what may happen afterward. It is both un-welcome and inevitable. Even Jesus was "greatly distressed and troubled (Mark 14:33, RSV)" when he had to face death.

There is a relationship between sin and death, especially in Paul's writings. But often this reference to death is in terms of separation, being "dead" to others, rather than

[2] *Hydriotaphia, Urne Buriall* (Boston: Houghton Mifflin Co., 1907), p. 41, cited in John P. Brantner, *Death Education,* ed. Betty R. Green and Donald P. Irish (Cambridge, Mass.: Schenkman, 1971), p. 17.

[3] *Ethic,* prop. 67, fourth part, *Spinoza Selections,* ed. John Wild (New York: Charles Scribner's Sons, 1930), p. 346.

physical death. Others write that death came into the world by way of sin, and is therefore seen as an enemy. For most people today it is quite clear that death is a natural and inevitable process and event, about which we cannot say very much, which would occur with or without sin.

For everything its season, and for every activity under heaven its time: a time to be born and a time to die (Eccles. 3:1–2, NEB).

But the time to die is frequently wrong, especially for the young. When death means that fulfillment is curtailed, plans are canceled, influence is stopped, or sacrifice is meaningless, we know that death is an enemy. Yet many young people face death with courage, faith, and hope. We will look closely at premature death later on. It is to be contrasted with death as fulfillment, at which time a person may not be ready or prepared for death; and yet beyond a certain age, as the psalmist says, "is their strength then but labour and sorrow; so soon passeth it away, and we are gone (Ps. 90:10, PB)."

ACQUAINTANCE WITH DEATH

Death is a kind of "absent presence" which flickers in the background of our thoughts, something on the horizon that is moving toward us at an undetermined speed.[4] "I know that I'm going to die, but I don't believe it," as Jacques Madaule wrote.[5] The idea of death hovers near the fringe of our consciousness, occasionally moving toward the center and then retreating. Occasionally it catches hold of us in a kind of compulsion and this leads to fear or dread or anxiety, but usually we can deal with its demand as a future event and it moves back to the outer rim of consciousness.

We do not have an immediate experience of death. "Death

---

[4] See Herman Feifel, *Death Education*, ed. Green and Irish, p. 3.
[5] Cited in Paul Danblon and André Godin, *Death and Presence*, ed. André Godin (Brussels: Lumen Vitae Press, 1972), p. 45. Used by permission.

is not an event in life," wrote Wittgenstein. "Death is not lived through."[6] If death consists of the loss of consciousness, and if the stopping of the brain functions is one clinical definition of death, then death cannot be part of experience. Reports from those who have been on the verge of death, or even clinically dead in some sense, are not clear and distinct but are more akin to reports of mystical experiences of wonder and light. We anticipate our own death because we observe it in others.

We can contemplate our own death, which is different from experiencing it, but we always contemplate it as outsiders. We reflect on it but we remain, so to speak, outside ourselves, visualizing our death or funeral or burial or cremation as an observer. When we define ourselves as ceasing to be, we remain the one who does the defining, so that there is a kind of duality of the self in this reflection that leads some people to think of an aspect of the self as transcending death.[7]

Our experience of death, then, is always indirect, based on our experience of the death of others, and this leads to equally indirect communication about the nature of death. We do not always apply this information to ourselves, or if we do it may reduce us to fear and anxiety.

Being in the presence of one who is expected to die brings out in us most of our feelings about death, and insofar as we seek to repress those emotions we seek to avoid the dying patient. This is a major reason why family members, doctors, and nurses are uncomfortable in the presence of someone who is about to die. They either refuse to enter a conversation dealing with oncoming death, escaping by various subterfuges from the topic, or else they simply avoid being in the patient's presence.

Another protection is indifference. If the experience of the deaths of others becomes too common, as in epidemics,

[6] Ludwig Wittgenstein, *Tractatus Logico-Philosophicus* (London: Kegan Paul, 1922), p. 185.
[7] See William E. Hocking, *Thoughts on Death and Life* (New York: Harper & Row, 1937), pp. 86–87.

disasters, or wars, those who survive often become insensitive as long as they, too, are not exposed to the same dangers. As long as someone a long way off, a stranger of another race, or even an unnamed person in an accident is involved, we retreat into a state of counting numbers and forget that human beings like ourselves are suffering and dying. Perhaps we need this impersonality tent to protect us from the overwhelming tragedy of multiple deaths of those of all ages in such catastrophes, but it leads to an indifference that approaches a less than human response. We only need to recall how belated was the response to the death of the many Jews under the Nazis, the willingness to let a war go on as long as Vietnamese rather than Americans were being killed, the difficulty of comprehending the deaths in Bangladesh from both tidal wave and war to realize how easy it is to reduce the deaths of others to statistics.

Our culture protects us from death. We simply do not see untreated dead persons; they are whisked away if they happen to die at home; or they die in hospitals and no one sees the body until it has been "prepared" for the funeral. We have moved far away from the experience described by Elisabeth Kübler-Ross:

I remember as a child the death of a farmer. He fell from a tree and was not expected to live. He asked simply to die at home, a wish that was granted without questioning. He called his daughters into the bedroom and spoke with each one of them alone for a few minutes. He arranged his affairs quietly, though he was in great pain, and distributed his belongings and his land, none of which was to be split until his wife should follow him in death. He also asked each of his children to share in the work, duties, and tasks that he had carried on until the time of the accident. He asked his friends to visit him once more, to bid good-bye to them. Although I was a small child at the time, he did not exclude me or my siblings. We were allowed to share in the preparations of the family just as we were permitted to grieve with them until he died. When he did die, he was left at home, in his own beloved home which he had built, and among his friends and neighbors who went to take a last look at him where he lay in the midst of flowers in the place he had lived in and loved so much.[8]

If one reflects on this old-fashioned scene, one can begin to see its values. Not only is the farmer enabled to die among friends and relatives, but he is cared for by those who understand his needs, preferences, and symptoms. He remains a person of significance until the end, rather than a semianonymous patient in a hospital. Furthermore, all those who surround him benefit from his experience, especially the children, who are included in the talk, fears, and grief of the family. It helps to give them a view of death that will stand them in good stead throughout their lives.

In many instances death was integrated with daily life. Today we have segregated death from life. Most people do not die at home, unless it is a sudden event. They are taken away to a hospital, and even in a hospital the dying and the dead are segregated from the living. When death occurs, it is treated as a secret. Sometimes those considered near death are removed to private rooms; bodies are never removed during visiting hours; and the morgue is often located where visitors will not notice it and where there is a private entrance for the hearse.[9]

There is a conspiracy of silence about death among doctors and nurses: they avoid the subject not only with the dying but also withhold information about the death of a patient from others. Of course, there are many exceptions to this custom among individual practitioners, but it is sufficiently documented by observers.[10] There is also evidence that nurses and doctors tend to avoid dying patients, and in some cases there is an expression of indifference when further medical care is deemed useless.

---

[8] Elisabeth Kübler-Ross, *On Death and Dying* (New York: Macmillan, 1969), pp. 5–6. Copyright © 1969 by Elisabeth Kübler-Ross. Used by permission of Macmillan Publishing Co., Inc.
[9] See Richard G. Dumont and Dennis C. Foss, *The American View of Death: Acceptance or Denial?* (Cambridge, Mass.: Schenkman, 1972), p. 37.
[10] See ibid., p. 39; Kübler-Ross, *On Death and Dying*, pp. 245–53.

Many of our funeral customs are a denial of the reality and finality of death. The casket is often constructed for protection against the elements and placed open in a "sleeping room." The cosmetic wizardry of the undertaker and the clothing are attempts to make the corpse look alive. The use of flowers in overwhelming abundance adds a touch of grotesquery and is often backed by strong economic pressure.[11] And at the grave, the casket is not lowered until the funeral party has left, so that they will not have to face the finality of watching the casket descending into the grave.

Our culture does not deal with death. There have been changes in recent years in such fields as humor, art, and literature so that references to death are deleted. If someone tries to make jokes about death, the response is similar to those about sex before the so-called sexual revolution. Death has replaced sex as a taboo topic. A content analysis of modern art indicates death is rarely the topic. It is true that death occurs in motion pictures and television shows, but it is usually treated impersonally or used to get rid of a person who is undesirable; and because there is no drawing in of the audience to the suffering and tragedy of death, one does not identify with the dying actor or actress as a person. Dumont and Foss conclude that "we find the American denial of death in our newspapers, movies, modern art, reaction to death statistics, humor, varied funeral customs and practices, use of euphemisms for death, children's games and literature, and treatment of the aged and dying."[12]

The treatment of the elderly is significant here. Because they are so often segregated from younger people, children rarely have the experience of seeing older people die. It is possible to live most of one's life without seeing a dead person or attending a funeral. We protect ourselves by sending the elderly to nursing homes or retirement communities, or they move, if they can afford it, to some "leisure world"

---

[11] Florists have been known to use economic boycotts of advertising to force newspapers to drop the notice "Please omit flowers." See Dumont and Foss, *The American View of Death*, pp. 40–41.

[12] Ibid., p. 43. Used by permission.

where everyone has time on his hands. Such people often find creative activities to occupy their time, but after four months a daily golf game or croquet or bridge or swimming begins to pall; and yet some kind of activity is the only escape from the realization that one is really on the shelf, no longer useful in a society still dominated by the work ethic. Early retirement only adds to the frustration. Many others, making do on small pensions, live in small apartments and count their pennies, and slowly withdraw into a world of their own. There may be values in sitting on a park bench on a pleasant day, but it does little for one's sense of worth. Nursing homes may be good or bad, and the bad ones provide no stimulus for meaningful living. But in all such cases the feeling of being segregated is often strong, and this leads to a lowering of morale.

Death may be in the offing for anyone at any age, but in the so-called golden years the coming of death may be sensed and yet denied. After all, medicine is making continuing strides toward longer life, and maybe science can get rid of even more seemingly incurable illnesses. Death may be inevitable, and yet it may seem farther off than it really is because of the miracles of science.

When one does admit that death is a possibility, some satisfaction may come from the knowledge that one lives on in his grandchildren, his contribution to business or society, or his ideas or his writings (as authors so fondly suppose). This "immortality of influence" has helped those who have come to doubt more traditional teachings about life after death. But now there is the possibility of a nuclear holocaust, which could bring to an end everything human and of value. Then there is no compensation except this life here and now, and although it is the place where we find meaning and value, we have not been taught to find it here. So we keep hoping for something beyond death.

There are those who have accepted the traditional teachings about heaven and hell, but this is not always helpful, because no one has the certainty of attaining heaven. If death means everlasting punishment, perhaps extinction would be preferable. So, if one sees negative value in an afterlife, as did the Jews in Sheol and the Greeks in Hades and the Hindus in reincarnation, there is a likelihood that one would deny death rather than face up to what comes afterwards.

There are those, however, who are confident that they will be with God in another world. When this is interpreted as immortality of the soul, it means that death is not final, for the soul goes on into a new existence and only the body is destroyed. This can be an article of faith and hope, but it also can be a form of denial of death. There is little evidence that convinced believers in immortality face death with any greater realism than nonbelievers.

Yet there are believers who face death and see it as fulfillment and victory. Some of these have a strong faith that they will live on in another world, or will inherit "eternal life" as something free from space and time but related to God. Others have a mature faith which enables them to accept death, but they see nothing beyond. So the issue actually is, How are we to face death? Until we see clearly what is involved rationally and emotionally in the inevitable fact of our own death, we will not be in a position to speak of hope beyond death. Once we have worked this out, then we may turn to the solution of the after-death situation.

There are many things that we seek to understand: Why is there such a widespread fear of death? What are the attitudes of children and adolescents toward death? What balance between acceptance and denial is healthy for us? What do we mean by a realistic view of death? When death is on the immediate horizon, do we want to know? How can we die with dignity in our culture? How is the church able to minister to the dying and what does it teach about death? What kind of hope can we have in relation to death? What is the meaning of life and death?

We will turn to these questions in succeeding chapters.

CHAPTER TWO

The Fear of Death

I believe that we should make it a habit to think about death and dying occasionally, I hope before we encounter it in our own life," writes Elisabeth Kübler-Ross.[1] Yet such thinking makes us uncomfortable because the fear of death is widespread if not universal.

We need to fear death. On the level of survival alone, fear of death is essential. If we had no fear of death, we would not take pains to avoid it. We need the protection of elemental fears in order to avoid the basic dangers to survival. We train children to recognize dangers of all kinds; we protect them from risks that they are unable to identify; we place poisons and medicines out of their reach; we supervise their play. Our alertness to what might happen protects us from carelessness as we become responsible for the lives of others. This kind of rational caution which we learned in childhood carries over into adult life. We know that one mistake can lead to death, and some of us have had narrow escapes.

This fear of death corresponds to a strong life instinct.

---

[1] Elisabeth Kübler-Ross, *On Death and Dying* (New York: Macmillan, 1969), p. 29. Copyright © 1969 by Elisabeth Kubler-Ross. Used by permission of Macmillan Publishing Co., Inc.

For most human beings life is a driving force even before it can be rationalized. Babies will struggle for survival as will animals. But life is soon sensed as important, and death is recognized as an enemy. Death wipes away the values and meaning of living, and as living is precious so dying is a threat, a work of evil, an act of Satan. In the Bible it is associated with sin, and the suggestion occurs that without sin, man would live forever. We simply are not ready to die, and so we fear this threat that never ceases to stand over us. We take whatever steps are necessary to insure survival in terms of health, avoidance of danger, and intelligent planning. This reaction is a normal and natural expression of the life instinct.

The fear of death has many other causes, especially in a culture that emphasizes the value of the individual rather than the common life. Our culture, supported by the Jewish and Christian concepts of the significance of the individual, places high value on personal achievement. Therefore death is the wiping out of all that a person stands for. Death means that one ceases to be, that there is a loss of identity as one becomes nothing. Paul Tillich has stressed the place of anxiety in the face of nonbeing; the finite self is threatened by nothingness and meaninglessness.

For others, death means perpetual isolation and loneliness. We rely so much on others for the meaning of our existence that we fear the loss of a supporting community. Just as solitary confinement is the worst of punishments, whether it is an experience of children locked in their rooms or of prisoners locked in their cells, so death is a form of isolation to be feared.

We value other people. Death means the loss of friends and family. Often the experience of death leads to grief not based on death but on the separation from those we love or depend on or support. Only in the case of very long lives when one outlives all one's human companions is this aspect of fear eliminated, but even extreme old age usually includes the experience of having someone around who cares.

We value our possessions. Just as older people do not like to sell their homes or give up other property when they move to smaller quarters or nursing homes, so death is a final loss of what we have stored up—like the man who had his excess possessions in ever-larger storehouses, who was told that "this very night you must surrender your life; you have made your money—who will get it now? (Luke 12:20, NEB)."

The fear of death is greatest among those between forty and sixty years of age. One reason for this is that they are in the prime of life, with many unfinished tasks, and they see death as a threat to the completion of their plans. Almost everyone has something uncompleted, but in middle life death is more costly in terms of responsibility to children and family, promotions on the job, changing roles for women as children leave home, enjoyment of grandchildren, and many other goals. There is much frustration when death threatens persons in those situations.

Death also leads to a sense of failure, especially in these same middle years. Terminal patients are likely to complain that they have failed their families, escaped their responsibilities, or let down their business partners by dying too young. A man may have failed to provide adequately for his widow and children; or a mother may wonder what will happen to her husband and children, for her death will wreck their family pattern.

There is a great deal of superstition about death. One may be haunted by the return of ghosts, by communication with mediums, or by the spookiness of cemeteries at night. Or one may be misled by ignorance about what experiences one may have after death, by a fear of worms eating the dead body in the ground or of feeling the fire in cremation or the knife in an autopsy. One may assume that the pain suffered prior to death will continue. Connected with this is the fear that one may be buried alive or that one's organs may be removed before one is dead, both of which are remote possibilities.

The fear of hell is real for many people. We find hell depicted in much medieval art, in the paintings in many cathedrals, and even in the Buddhist Tiger Balm Garden in Singapore. Much fundamentalist preaching, both Protestant and Catholic, has included vivid pictures of hell. Ignace Lepp tells of a recent sermon in which the preacher in a sort of ecstasy shouted: "I see him . . . I see him. . . . How horrible. . . . He is burning in Hell. . . . The devil sneers and attacks." Lepp comments: "I later learned that the subject of this horrifying vision was a recently deceased archbishop of Paris who was guilty, in the eyes of the integralists, of favoring social reform in Leon Blum's government in 1936."[2] There is some carry-over of traditional views of hell in the imaginations of many of us, so that we not only enjoy jokes about hell but keep the vision of it in our minds as we contemplate death with an uncanny feeling of dread.

Religion often increases the fear of death through its visions of the future, either of unending bliss or unending torture, with the possibility of a period of testing to decide which way one may be going. Death in a very real sense is not considered the end of finite existence, and the idea of any kind of timelessness is frightening. Yet the idea of being with God in some kind of future existence may also be satisfying enough to provide confidence in the face of death. It is difficult, however, to establish whether religion is the result of one's attitude toward death or the cause of it. It is probable, as Robert Fulton says, that religion "plays a dual role in a person's attitude toward death. Religion for the deeply devout person may be 'functional' and supportive, or it may be 'dysfunctional.' "[3]

We have no empirical evidence of what happens in death. All we have is a dead body to be disposed of in some suitable manner following traditional religious or cultural lines.

[2] Ignace Lepp, *Death and Its Mysteries* (New York: Macmillan, 1968), p. 67. Used by permission.

[3] Robert L. Fulton, ed., *Death and Identity* (New York: John Wiley & Sons, 1965), p. 81. Used by permission.

Death leads to fear of the unknown, for we do not know when we will die or what the experience means except that we will cease to *be* in any sense that can be observed by others. We have no reputable evidence from the other side of the grave, although some of us are eager to believe the reports from spiritualists or other seers. It is somewhat easier for terminal patients who are told they will die, for at least the uncertainty of the nearness of death is removed, but even they are not freed from the fear of the unknown that death itself provides.

Finally, to this list of the causes of the fear of death should be added the fear of being taken by surprise. Although many people say they would prefer a sudden death, as in an accident, a traditional petition in the prayer called the litany includes the request to be spared "from sudden death." But even when death is a normal happening, the patient is taken by surprise and is likely to respond with a "No, it cannot be I." Almost all premature death includes this element of being surprised at its early occurrence.

The fear of death, we have said, serves a positive function in helping us to stay alive and protecting us from those activities that might terminate life. Such fear, when held in proper perspective, is not only normal and rational but necessary. But it is not a simple one-dimensional response. It is, as Gardner Murphy says, "a very complex thing with conscious, preconscious, and unconscious aspects and all sorts of predetermining cultural and religious factors."[4] In everyone there is a complex mixture of emotional responses to the prospect of death, and often only the surface ones can be articulated as we have done. Even those who give no impression of fearing death may have a hidden and deep-seated emotional dread. Others may be relatively free of overt or hidden fears and are free to operate in terms of both a meaningful life and an appreciation of the art of dying.

---

[4] Gardner Murphy, *The Meaning of Death*, ed. Herman Feifel (New York: McGraw-Hill, 1959), p. 335. Used by permission.

ANXIETY AND DEATH

Fear and anxiety are much alike in that both are uncanny and unpleasant emotions approaching dread. Psychologists tell us that the difference is that fear has an object and that anxiety does not, so that we can deal with our fears and not with our anxieties. Paul Tillich accepts this definition. We can fear being killed or being in a fatal accident, but death means that we cease to be; and this nonbeing or nothing is not an object, and therefore creates anxiety. So we are anxious about the fact that we will become nothing.[5]

We need to transform this anxiety into fear but cannot do so. Simply to be human means to be anxious about ceasing to be. Tillich finds the answer to this problem in what he calls "the courage to be," which means that we have faith that we are accepted as we are by God.[6] If Tillich is right, there is still no easy way to his proposed solution. It involves a struggle, even after one is accepted and the power of being moves in on our anxiety about our nonbeing; so that finally Tillich concludes his thesis with this: *"The courage to be is rooted in the God who appears when God has disappeared in the anxiety of doubt."*[7]

If anxiety cannot be changed to fear by taking death seriously and realistically, it can do a great deal of damage. If we turn from Tillich's treatment of anxiety to a more psychological interpretation, we discover that anxiety about anything, because it has no object that can be dealt with, precipitates the anxious person in the direction of what he is anxious about. We find this with accident-prone people, with those who in their anxiety find their experiences culminating in the very results that they did not desire. In the case of anxiety about death, it can precipitate death. "Anxious fear of death," says Lepp, "paralyzes action, renders man unsuited for life, and sometimes even deprives him of

[5] Paul Tillich, *The Courage to Be* (New Haven: Yale University Press, 1952), pp. 37–38.
[6] Ibid., p. 166.
[7] Ibid., p. 190.

the desire to live. Fear, as we have seen, serves life; but anxiety serves death."[8] Suicide and sometimes murder can result from neurotic anxiety about death.

The Bible in some of its books promises the end of the world, a collective death of all living creatures. It is an idea or fixation growing out of primitive man's experience with floods, earthquakes, famines, and plagues, mixed with prophetic judgment on the immoral aspects of a culture. It exists in what Jung calls the collective unconscious, and is found in non-Christian cultures as well. It keeps occurring in the expectations of various sects, who set the date and then readapt quickly when Jerusalem does not fall or Jesus does not come.

Yet there is a sense in which cultures have died. If Toynbee is right, there have been twenty-one civilizations or cultures, all of which have disintegrated. But the people have not perished from the earth and Christ has not returned; so that ends of culture, although reflecting a similar principle, are not parallel to the destruction of the apocalypse.

However, in the twentieth century man controls the means for obliterating humankind and all living creatures through the use of nuclear bombs. This has led to a pervasive fear that operates in the unconscious and often surfaces in particular decisions, such as not to marry or have children (precisely as in Paul's advice in New Testament times). This fear is often repressed, but one can observe its effect in the breakdown in morality, the insistence on pleasure now, and on the "eat, drink, and be merry, for tomorrow we die" philosophy. Lepp observes that this fear is most obvious in those countries which have nuclear weapons. There is no sense of security.[9]

A secular apocalyptic has been substituted for a religious one, but in both cases there is the threat of extinction. Only, in the case of religion, true believers assume they will some-

---

[8] Lepp, *Death and Its Mysteries,* p. 47.
[9] Ibid., pp. 60–64.

how survive death others deserve. We have no guarantee life will continue on earth, and to this extent both kinds of apocalyptists are right. Without a nuclear holocaust or divine intervention there will come a time when earth cannot support life. Thus the values that are developed by any civilization are doomed ultimately to extinction.

But this does not change our fundamental thesis: fear of death in its subordinate place is an important element in creative and meaningful living; neurotic or compulsive fear of death, and especially anxiety about death, gets in the way of what it means to be human, with all the richness of human relationships that makes this life worth living.

FEAR OF DYING

Dying can be a long drawn out process, it can be swift and painless, or it can be somewhere in between. Since all life is becoming and perishing, in one sense we are dying all the time as we move toward death from birth. But as the days go by, this experience of becoming and perishing moves toward the expectation that our days are numbered. We then enter into a process where the perishing outweighs the becoming, and we see the end approaching.

There are people who have only a normal fear of death but may have a strong fear of the process of dying. Death we do not have to live through, but dying is a process which is part of living, with the pain and suffering that accompany it.

So people properly fear the process of dying. There is the problem of facing death as such, which we will discuss in chapter 6, but this problem is to be seen now in terms of what is anticipated concerning what happens prior to death. Often this is related to cancer, because it is a painful and long drawn out experience, but it can be related to other illnesses such as multiple sclerosis or arthritis. The fear of this kind of dying is illustrated in the discovery that people want to die in their own bed in their sleep, but they want to avoid a sudden death for which there is no preparation. A relatively painless death for which one is enabled to be ready is desired. Yet many people are afflicted with lengthy terminal diseases.

What people fear in the process of dying is first of all the pain. Modern drugs can control much of the pain, but often at the expense of certain side effects. What is especially galling is the experience of dependency, relying on others for basic needs. This is particularly difficult for those who have been self-reliant or whose help comes from family members or nurses who resent the demands on them.

Others fear the loss of their appearance. It is hard to look well groomed when one is ill, and in a long sickness there are changes as one loses weight or is disfigured due to operations. This often leads to a loss of dignity as well, especially when one is treated in an impersonal or indifferent manner. This may lead to a sense of shame for being ill and a sense of helplessness. One may feel as if one is treated as dead before the death takes place.

Finally, there is the sense of being alone, not in the satisfying sense of solitariness and communion with God, but in the sense of being neglected. It is true that no one can do our dying for us and we have to die alone, but in the process of dying we need the loving support of family, friends, and staff, who in some cases are so uncomfortable in their knowledge of our approaching death that they cannot bring themselves to enter meaningful personal relationships.

These are realistic fears: pain, dependency, loss of appearance, loss of dignity, shame, impersonal treatment, and loneliness. To die with dignity is a right that the fact of being human gives us, and we will look at this in chapter 7.

THE DEATH WISH

Is there a death wish or death instinct? Freud thought there was. He used the word *thanatos* for it, and the whole study of death is now called *thanatology*. There seems to be enough evidence for us to say that most people at some time in their lives have had the wish to die, not in the sense of suicide, but only an "I wish I were dead" response to frustration or disappointment. This death wish may be expressed unconsciously in unwitting choices and actions, such as accident proneness, actions to guarantee failure, drug addiction, intoxication, certain depressive states, excessive risk taking, and even the way we drive automobiles or motorcycles. Some antisocial behavior may be indicative of the death wish. When there is a strong dislike of life, or when one's values are in disarray, or when meaninglessness is asserted as the interpretation of life, this may be an expression of the death wish. Religious teachings usually stress the positive side of life, and some have concluded that the death wish is stronger among irreligious people. There are some who think it is stronger among women than among men.[10]

There is no universal agreement with Freud about the death wish. Some psychologists carry this theory to the extreme by applying it to a child's refusal to eat, saving a person from drowning, military valor, nursing contagious diseases, heroism at a fire, or driving a race car. Human beings do risk their lives, but many reasons other than a death instinct can be called upon to explain their actions. Lepp believes that Freud's theory of a death wish derives from his pessimism rather than from clinical observation.[11] The truth probably lies somewhere in the middle.

RELIGION

Epicurus, writing in the third century before Christ, faced the problem of death with great simplicity: "Where we are, death is not yet; and where death comes, there we are not." He saw the fear of death as due to the fear of the gods and of life after death, especially of hell. Death puts an end to

[10] See Richard G. Dumont and Dennis C. Foss, *The American View of Death: Acceptance or Denial?* (Cambridge, Mass.: Schenkman, 1972), pp. 24–28.
[11] See Lepp, *Death and Its Mysteries,* p. 37.

suffering and evil as well as to pleasure; therefore it is nothing to be feared. Life is meaningful because it provides pleasure, although pleasure of a highly sophisticated sort. So we do not need to worry about death.

At the opposite pole, the Stoics saw the universe as good and reason as the basis for living. They took things in their stride and did not waver from the path of virtue. God is the rational soul of the world. A man looks on death or a comedy with the same unemotional countenance. So one lives in the present, does his duty, and refuses to let his imagination operate to confuse him about the future. Therefore, he does not fear death but takes it in stride as a natural and rational event.

Traditional Christianity has always emphasized the significance of human life, both on earth and hereafter. But there has been an erosion of faith, and, as James Reston has pointed out, this has led to a kind of pessimism:

With the decline of religious faith, there has already come a decline in the belief in the sanctity of human life. Without this essentially religious view that each human being is a unique and precious symbol of some kind of divine order, it is easier to regard the universe as merely a great machine, pointlessly grinding its way toward ultimate stagnation and death.[12]

This loss of religious faith, which we can document especially in terms of life after death, is a challenge to the churches to change their approach to death education, especially in terms of building Christian attitudes toward death long before it is an immediate threat. If it can be shown that religion at present makes no difference in the way people face death, as some investigators believe,[13] there is much to be done.

---

[12] *New York Times,* May 31, 1970, p. 14E, © 1970 by The New York Times Company. Reprinted by permission. Cited in Betty R. Green and Donald P. Irish, eds., *Death Education* (Cambridge, Mass.: Schenkman, 1971), p. 63.
[13] See André Godin, ed., *Death and Presence* (Brussels: Lumen Vitae Press, 1972), pp. 228–29.

Death has often been related to sin, so that anyone who is dying young asks, "What did I do to deserve this?" The fact that most saints die young never seems to occur to such theologians. Sin, as interpreted by Paul, leads to separation from God and our fellows, and this is "death" in only a figurative sense. As long as villains live to be ninety and saints die at thirty-three, we who take evidence seriously will have to ask the church to recast some of its teaching about the relation of sin and death.

We will see later that it is possible to relate belief in a good God to death as a natural event, without doing violence to God's goodness or the necessity for death. We will still have the problem of the time of death and the way in which death occurs, whether by illness, accident, war, or murder.

Religion may either increase or decrease the fear of death, or do both at the same time. "The anxious person finds new reasons for anxiety in his religion; the more secure person also derives from his religion the means of justifying his security," so preaching about hope for eternal life is always problematic.[14]

SEX AS COVERUP

Rollo May suggests that our preoccupation with sex at every level of life is an obsession that moderates our anxiety about death.

When I strive to prove my potency in order to cover up and silence my inner fears of impotence, I am engaging in a pattern as ancient as man himself. Death is the symbol of ultimate impotence and finiteness, and anxiety arising from this inescapable experience calls forth the struggle to make ourselves infinite by way of sex. Sexual activity is the most ready way to silence

---

[14] Ibid., p. 229. Used by permission.

the inner dread of death and, through the symbol of procreation, to triumph over it.[15]

So potency becomes a symbol of life and we strive to keep this potency active. When this potency dies or one begins to fear the oncoming of sexual impotence, he may lose the will to live. May points out that this is what happened to Ernest Hemingway, who took his own life. The sex instinct takes over from the life instinct in order to repress the fact of death, and as sexual potency fails before life does, one becomes helpless in the face of death.

CONCLUSION

The fear of death is normal provided we keep it in the background without repressing it. As we face death, our fears can be alleviated if we do not lose social support at the same time; it is bearable when we have not lost the capacity to love and the opportunity to be loved.

The willingness to live must be matched with the willingness to die. As Hocking wrote, "Property is not mine until I can alienate it; life is not mine until I can renounce it."[16] This means that we can take risks, even of our lives, in order to achieve what is worthwhile. We discover that we can live meaningfully with the fear of death, and in a sense overcome it. This is what Tagore meant when he wrote about the airplane as a victory of the spirit: "For it was not until, in the West, man had overcome the fear of death that he could master the art of flying—the art of the Gods!"[17]

---

[15] Rollo May, *Love and Will* (New York: W. W. Norton & Co., 1969), p. 106. Used by permission. See 1 Kings 1:1–4.
[16] William E. Hocking, *Thoughts on Death and Life* (New York: Harper & Row, 1937), p. 25. Used by permission.
[17] Cited in ibid., p. 26.

CHAPTER THREE

Children and Death

One way in which we can understand our attitude toward death is to recall how we felt as children, for we carry over many such emotional reactions into our adult life. Some of this information can be obtained from those adults who can remember the more vivid of their early death experiences, and there is now a good deal of research among children which gives us some accurate pictures of how they respond to death.

Although many children today are isolated from death and far fewer children die than in former years, death is still an element in the process of growing up. It appears in various forms in the thinking and experience of even very young children. Of course, their conception of death is different as they move from one stage to another. Maria Nagy has identified three stages, and although children do not fit neatly into these categories, it helps us to identify the development of children in terms of an overall view.

CHILDREN TO ABOUT AGE FIVE

A certain percentage of nursery rhymes deal with death, often in terms of murder.

> Fee, fi, fo, fum,
> I smell the blood of an Englishman.
> Be he live or be he dead,
> I'll grind his bones to make my bread.

Or this one:

> Solomon Grundy,
> Born on Monday,
> Died on Saturday,
> Buried on Sunday,
> And this is the end
> Of Solomon Grundy.

Or the familiar:

> "Who killed Cock Robin?"
> "I," said the sparrow,
> "With my bow and arrow.
> I killed Cock Robin."

And even more vividly:

> The end of oranges and lemons
> Say the bells of St. Clemens. . . .
> Here comes a candle to light you to bed;
> Here comes a chopper to chop off your head.

John Brantner also quotes an African lullaby:

> Twist his neck and hit him on the head,
> Throw him in the ditch and he'll be dead.[1]

Children *like* these rhymes. They ask for them repeatedly, and they will laugh or cringe or even cry in delight. Many children learned the prayer:

> Now I lay me down to sleep,
> I pray thee, Lord, my soul to keep.
> If I should die before I wake,
> I pray thee, Lord, my soul to take.

This prayer relates death and sleep, which is a common enough association, but if the child for some reason already

---

[1] John P. Brantner, *Death Education*, ed. Betty R. Green and Donald P. Irish (Cambridge, Mass.: Schenkman, 1971), pp. 16–17. Used by permission.

has some anxiety about either death or the dark, this prayer is hardly reassuring.

More games are related to death than we may suspect. For example, Ring-around-the-rosy, a delightful game, arose during the bubonic plague in medieval Europe. Joining hands was the ritual of life, but in the ritual of movement suddenly "all fall down!" This was a realistic playing at death, with the fortunate consequence that all could rise again. The game of Dead Man Arise also starts with death, as the "corpse" lies on the ground and the children mourn over him. Suddenly he jumps up and the children freeze or scatter, and the one caught becomes Dead Man for the next round.[2] Cowboys and Indians is a game where after the "Bang, you're dead" everything returns to normal. Death is not permanent but is more like temporary banishment.

Young children do not have the exposure to death in today's conditions that they had even fifty years ago. The changes in medical skills have lessened the mortality rate of infants as well as older people; the place of dying is more likely to be away from home and children; and many children do not attend funerals. As a result, they neither see nor touch dead bodies. They may hear about the deaths of people they know; they witness death in the mass media; and they know about sudden deaths from accidents. This lack of contact with death eliminates direct experience but does not affect the "absent presence" of death in children's consciousness, for they still act out their fantasies about death and within their limitations of mental construction think about it.

Often the first direct contact with death may be with a pet or an animal in the yard. Robert Kastenbaum tells of how his eighteen-month-old boy, David, found a dead bird. He was puzzled, but made no attempt to touch it. His countenance changed from discovery to puzzlement to tragedy. For several mornings he would stop and look at the dead

---

[2] See Robert Kastenbaum, "The Kingdom Where Nobody Dies," *Saturday Review,* Dec. 23, 1972, p. 34.

bird. A few weeks later he discovered a second dead bird, and his reaction was different. He picked it up and gestured that he wanted it returned to its limb on the tree. His father tried to explain, but the child insisted. But of course the bird did not fly. Later he had a similar experience with a fallen leaf. David could recognize a problem associated with death, and he sought to reverse the condition, setting in motion the processes of curiosity and questioning that make learning possible.[3]

If death occurs and the child is involved, it may increase his fear of death. Fear of the corpse, especially if it is touched after it is cold, is an important factor. The whole situation, with casket, grief reactions among adults, and misleading explanations can add to his fear. Yet it is worse if he is kept away from a family experience of death and grief, because he senses the atmosphere and is shunted aside at the same time.

Some children may give indications of the fear of death as early as the age of three, and others show no evidence of it at all. Some experiences of death seem to make no impression; others, as in David's case, arouse curiosity but not fear; and others may stimulate anxiety, frustration, and even rage. It is important that adults avoid some of the easy and misleading answers to his questions, especially if he has experienced the death of a parent or sibling. He should never be told that someone has gone on a long voyage. Even to be told that someone has gone to heaven or has been taken by Jesus may cause great resentment or the fear that the "ghost" may return sometime. The use of the euphemism that someone has fallen asleep may result in the child's terror at going to sleep at night.[4]

Young children think about death, but they are unable to conceptualize it because their thinking is still, in Piaget's categories, preoperational. They cannot distinguish between

[3] Ibid., p. 37.
[4] André Godin, ed., *Death and Presence* (Brussels: Lumen Vitae Press, 1972), pp. 194–95.

fact and fantasy, they cannot see connections between events, and therefore they distort much of what they are told. In their fantasies, death appears as a factor, even when the original situation would not suggest it to an adult. They usually think of death as something which happens to an adult. A four-year-old may say, "I don't want to grow up because when you do, you die."[5] The child under five does not think of death as definite; someone may eat or drink or grow in his coffin. Death is gradual so that there may be activities in the grave and in heaven; and death is reversible.

He reasons in a magical way and therefore he sees no connection between cause and effect except that his wishes might come true. So when he wishes for the death of someone as a result of his frustration in the process of becoming socialized, he becomes fearful that someone may wish for his death, too. Yet he does not contemplate his own death, and he sees no connection between either chance or a natural happening and death.[7]

Especially with young children but also with children generally, parents do not discuss death in any helpful way. They may be forced to face the topic when death strikes close to home, but often evasive answers are given. Such evasion and deception are probably due to parental anxiety about death, which leads to anxiety in the children. Parents who have been emancipated enough to do a fairly good job of sex education are still full of Victorian prudery about the subject of death. Yet the child is going to hear about war, violence, and accidents leading to death; he is likely to have toys of destruction; and his games are used to express all kinds of fantasies about death. He needs help in establishing helpful attitudes, and parents who already have a healthy attitude may share it with their children. At this age, religious concepts are not particularly helpful, primarily because

---

[5] Herman Feifel, *Death Education,* ed. Green and Irish, p. 5.

[6] See Maria H. Nagy, "The Child's View of Death," *The Meaning of Death,* ed. Herman Feifel (New York: McGraw-Hill, 1959), pp. 81–88.

[7] See Charles W. Wahl, "The Fear of Death," *Death and Identity,* ed. Robert Fulton (New York: John Wiley & Sons, 1965), pp. 62–65.

the child cannot grasp them. Heaven is simply a place to which the dead person journeys, and he may return. If Jesus took away the child's mother, then Jesus is seen as an enemy. Even the statement that God loves him does not help a child unless he is being loved all the time by his parents.

After the Lindbergh kidnapping in 1932, Billy was told that Charlie was away from home; later, after the body was found, Billy was told that Charlie was dead. Billy asked no questions, but about a year later (when he was four), he told his father that he had figured it out:

About Charlie. You see, he got lost in the woods. And a kind airman came along and found him. He picked him up and put him in his airplane. He flew away up into the sky. When he couldn't fly any higher God opened the sky. He let a rope down. The airman tied the rope around Charlie and God pulled him up right into the sky beside him.[8]

Because this is Billy's own thinking and is reassuring to him, it is well to let it alone. The telling of this story indicates Billy's security with his own parents, and perhaps that is the way God works with children. Charles W. Wahl puts it this way:

The child who is strongly dependent upon his significant adults for his security and his conception of himself as a worthy and adequate person is capable, if they meet these needs, of integrating the concept of "not-being" if his parents can do so, and he is solaced by the thought that his demise (and theirs) is yet far away.[9]

This is the kind of reassurance that is both human and religious, and from it the child as he gets older may handle views of what happens after death on his own terms.

[8] Mildred and Frank Eakin, *Your Child's Religion* (New York: Macmillan, 1942), p. 48. Used by permission.
[9] Wahl, *Death and Identity,* ed. Fulton, p. 65. Quoted from the *Bulletin of the Menninger Clinic,* 22, pp. 214–23. © the Menninger Foundation, 1958. Used by permission.

THE CHILD FROM SIX TO NINE

Some children grasp the reality of death at an early age, but they usually fluctuate between seeing it as reversible and seeing it as final. Between the ages of five and nine, according to the research of Maria Nagy, they begin to see death as an enemy, personified in various ways, as an angel or clown or skeleton. He operates at night and comes at us from the outside. He may be the "boogieman," which is why it is not wise to shut up children in closets where the "boogieman" might get them. Death operates invisibly and in secret. As long as we can escape the death man we are safe. Death, however, is not seen as final.[10]

There is no element of chance in the child's thinking. Death is evil-intentioned and personified for most children of this age, but there is no natural cause of death, except the wishing and thinking that make it so.

About the age of eight or nine, death is seen as an irreversible fact, as a cessation of all bodily activities, and as an organic process obeying organic laws.[11] They are ready to move, at about age eleven, into more abstract considerations of death as a concept to be understood, but this rational capacity to think accurately about the nature of death may have no impact on their emotional response to the idea.

It might add to our understanding if we examine the results of research on children in relation to the assassination of President Kennedy, the shock and period of mourning, and the funeral ceremonies on TV. The younger children were upset primarily because of sharing in their parents' grief. Among both kindergarten and third-grade children there was an upsurge in aggressive imagery, so that their stories were focused on themes of killings, violence, and hospitals. They were highly stimulated by what they saw on TV and could not control their behavior. It was, however, highly educational, especially for the younger children, in

[10] See Nagy, *The Meaning of Death,* ed. Feifel, pp. 88–96.
[11] See Godin, ed., *Death and Presence,* pp. 144–45.

helping them to accept the finality of death for both good and bad people. But there was still a great deal of denial, and some children did not become convinced for about three or four months that Kennedy was really dead and would not return.[12]

But what of the dying child? Such a premature death offers a challenge to everyone's faith, for here is the cutting off of potentiality and fulfillment in an arbitrary manner. We do not know how much a small child knows about what is happening, but it seems as if there is a sense of death although little realization of what it means. He has no capacity for imagining what it means to cease to be. Various influences are working on him, including the attitudes and beliefs of his family. If they are fatalistic and anxious, he is likely to become so. If they have placed emphasis on life after death, he may think of it as a great adventure.

Whatever forebodings adults around him may have, he is likely to realize vaguely that they apply to him. He will sense their sadness and grief. But he may rise above the level of adults and may say to his nurse, "Let's talk about my death for a moment while Mommy isn't here." An adolescent dying of tuberculosis said, "Please explain to my parents that it was far better for me to die." Another said, "Don't discuss it with my family. They're already so downhearted."[13]

There are ways to let a child know he is dying without being too blunt and brutal and without giving a time limit. There are ways to help him talk about death both medically and pastorally, and this can be helpful both to the dying child and to his parents.

ADOLESCENCE

When the adolescent structures his life, death stands outside the mainstream. He may see it as a future threat, but

---

[12] See ibid., pp. 153–54.
[13] Quoted in Godin, ed., *Death and Presence,* p. 210.

it does not emerge as a part of his overall way of thinking. He lives intensely in the present, with past and future as insignificant or even unpleasant. Because there is so much else to occupy his consciousness, one would not expect him to focus on death, but it may lead to some difficult adjustments later in life if there is not some way of structuring the meaning of death into his overall outlook. A small percentage of youth with religious backgrounds keep death in perspective and seem to have a healthier outlook.[14]

But death crowds in on the adolescent as it does with children and adults. There are friends who are killed in accidents or on the playing field; there are cancer patients in their teens; there are young men in the armed forces. Just because one does not focus on death when talking of his life plans does not mean that he is not going to think about it from time to time. Furthermore, today's world stands under the threat of nuclear disaster and young people know it. It affects their plans for marriage and having children, for education and work, for pleasure and leisure, often in a negative way. There is an apocalyptic note in the chorus of our anthems of life.

It is normal for adolescents to have a sense of invulnerability. It is part of the charm of youth. A confidence that young people can remake the world may strike some older people as arrogance, but in the past it has been the supreme confidence of youthful leaders that has helped to make the world a better place. However, there is a fluctuation of temperament, and these same young people have a sense of impending disaster, not only from nuclear weapons but from a reading of the signs of the times, so that many of them see the beginning of the doom of Western civilization.

Furthermore, young people do die. Although the death rate for ages fifteen to twenty-four has gone down since 1900 from about 5.8 to 1.4 per thousand white males, which is among the lowest rates for any age group, there are still

---

[14] See Feifel, ed., *The Meaning of Death*, pp. 99–113.

a number of deaths. Some die without knowing what happened, but others suffer from fatal illnesses and know that they are going to die. There are stories of how some young persons have handled themselves and consoled their family and friends in such situations. But we do not have hard evidence on enough of them to make definite statements.

DEATH EDUCATION

When should we start death education? Certainly the death-bed is far too late. It has been suggested that we need to start death education as we have learned to begin sex education, making it part of the whole process of learning at those points where it is relevant. Marjorie Mitchell writes: "As children grow up it should be natural for us to tell them all we know about death scientifically and philosophically."[15] The goal should be to help children and adults "understand their own feelings and attitudes toward death and dying so that death will be less fearful and living more enjoyable."[16]

Certain elements in death education are obvious. First, it should be a continuing process but also intermittent. No one can look at death for any length of time without distorting his view of life. Second, in spite of the earlier realism about death in olden days, we cannot simply try to return to those practices even if it were possible; we need to combine realism with the findings of modern research and operate in terms of today's values. Third, today's realism needs to be modified by avoidance and denial procedures, so that the threat of death does not predominate. Fourth, because we are primarily interested in living, ways of avoiding death, health measures, and safety instructions need to be brought to bear on the constructive use of the fear of death. Fifth, suicide needs to be included as part of our understanding of the death wish. Sixth, religious teachings are relevant to most approaches to the meaning of death.

---

[15] Godin, ed., *Death and Presence*, p. 203. Used by permission.
[16] Green and Irish, eds., *Death Education*, p. 30.

It is obvious that some teaching about death, either good or bad, will occur in family and church. But when it is proposed that death education be included in the school curriculum, objections are likely to arise from those in the community who think that death is a topic to be repressed. The battle over death education has been likened to that over sex education, in that both are taboo topics. Furthermore, both sex and death are surrounded by private value systems that are challenged by any kind of objective teaching. Both topics are highly charged emotionally. There is resistance to any nonmoral or nonvalue approach to sex or death, and yet any value system that may be used is open to question by many people.

There are those who believe that objective teaching on controversial issues, which include religion and politics as well as sex and death, can include a variety of options in terms of interpretation and value judgment. But this takes a teacher with special skills not unlike the teacher of sex or religion. According to Warren Johnson and Daniel Leviton, some of the preliminary criteria might be:

1. The teacher needs to have worked out his or her own view of death as part of "the dynamics of his own personality functioning."

2. He needs to have mastered the subject matter.

3. He must be at ease in using language about death.

4. He must be able to see the role that consciousness of death plays in the developmental psychology of the growing person.

5. He needs to be aware of the tremendous changes taking place in our culture in relation to social, moral and religious thinking concerning death.[17]

These same criteria might well be suggested for the parent or church school teacher dealing with the subject of

[17] See Daniel Leviton, *Death Education,* ed. Green and Irish, p. 39; Warren R. Johnson, *Human Sexual Behavior and Sex Education,* 2d ed. (Philadelphia: Lea & Febiger, 1968), p. 13.

death, and they would serve as an approach to the meaning of death for all of us.

Death education in the schools demands a sensitivity that makes possible response to existential issues about death. If death education opens up hidden suicidal tendencies, some kind of counseling should be available. If deaths occur that affect the students, those particular deaths need to be handled within the school framework. The concern is to assist persons to handle their death fears and anxieties in such a way that they can live meaningfully in the present. Often this can be done by examining the deaths of various heroes, looking back to Lincoln or King or Kennedy who were assassinated or to Roberto Clemente or Hale Boggs or Will Rogers who died in airplane crashes.

People can be helped if they realize that it is all right both to deny and to accept the reality of death, for this can lead to a realistic view of death as it fits today's world. In this perspective, they can face up to the way in which people may respond when they know that death is certain within a limited time. At this point, we can talk about dying with dignity and planning our own death and funeral in an intelligent manner. For many of us, this brings in the question of the role of church or synagogue and its ministry to the dying. When we have come to terms with death with these understandings, we can talk about hope and the variety of ways in which death is seen as meaningful, both with and without a view of the afterlife. Finally, all this can be comprehended within a universe in which a loving God is working to make our lives meaningful.[18]

Let us turn to the acceptance-denial hypothesis.

---

[18] I have written briefly about children and death in *Your Child's Religion* (Garden City: Doubleday, 1962), pp. 124–27; *The Clue to Christian Education* (New York: Charles Scribner's Sons, 1950), pp. 192–200; *Biblical Theology and Christian Education* (New York: Charles Scribner's Sons, 1956), pp. 156–66.

CHAPTER FOUR

Acceptance and Denial

In one of the most informative books on death, *The American View of Death: Acceptance or Denial?* by Richard G. Dumont and Dennis C. Foss,[1] the authors develop what they call the "acceptance-denial hypothesis." They examine carefully the evidence for the denial of death in contemporary culture, contrast it with the evidence for acceptance of death, and then conclude that we must allow for varying degrees of denial or acceptance, or both, and that we must also look for both witting and unwitting responses at a variety of levels.[2]

It is probable that much of our denial of death is a way of handling our fear of death. By simply cutting death out of our consciousness, we can act and think as if we will continue to live indefinitely. We make our plans within the scheme of the relatively near future, and put the later future out of mind.

Some of us do the opposite. In the light of certain religious or philosophical beliefs, we believe that we will live forever and that therefore death is not real or final. This

---

[1] Cambridge, Mass.: Schenkman, 1972.
[2] Ibid., p. 107.

guarantee of immortal existence enables us to live in this temporary body without thinking about death. Until recently, perhaps the majority of Christians and many Jews accepted belief in some kind of afterlife. It may be, as we will consider in chapter 9, that there are good reasons for hope of some kind of afterlife, but from the psychological point of view an *unexamined* belief in immortality is a form of denial of death. If one's attitude toward death is primarily one of denial, and if support for that denial is an unexamined and uncritical belief, then we are dealing with what Wahl calls "magical thinking and delusion formation."[3] The question is whether one derives certain beliefs as a compensation for fear, and thus denies that death is real, or whether one is able to face the reality of death and then come to conclusions about life after death on the basis of religious or philosophical presuppositions. The Christian approach, it might be said here, has always started with the reality and finality of death, and only in the light of the reality of death has it moved to belief in resurrection. The popular view that the soul does not die is a distortion of Christian belief.

There are many practices in our culture which support the denial of death. Individuals may not conform to cultural expectations, and therefore many people have found other approaches to an understanding of death, but these cultural factors play a large part in the formation of attitudes toward death.

There is a taboo on death as a subject for conversation. If we have to talk about it, we say that someone "passed on" or has "gone to a better realm" but never that he "died." Undertakers first became "funeral directors" and then "morticians" and now "grief specialists," who place the dead in a "sleeping room." In fact, "the loved one" never had it so good, with all the cosmetics to hide death and clothing to

---

[3] Charles W. Wahl, "The Fear of Death," *Death and Identity*, ed. Robert Fulton (New York: John Wiley & Sons, 1965), p. 58. Quoted from the *Bulletin of the Menninger Clinic*, 22, pp. 214–23, © The Menninger Foundation, 1958. Used by permission.

make the body ready for a ride to somewhere. Funeral practices and rituals are important to help us accept the reality of death and to work out our grief, but we need reality rather than false assurances in order for this to come to pass.

Even the convenient practice of letting undertakers take over and make all the arrangements is a way of avoiding death. Many of the functions of the funeral director used to be those of the family, but now the body is removed immediately and is not seen again until it appears in the casket, resting on fine satin in a magnificent setting.

In reaction against this and ignoring the values inherent in many funeral practices, some groups have moved away from tradition. Not only has the idea of gift giving at the time of death been dropped by many people, but the time of grief has been foreshortened, so that there is little time to contemplate either the death of the one who has died or the meaning of death for the bereaved before one is back to life as usual.

Memorial societies have come into being with the exemplary idea of simplifying funerals. They have advocated lower costs, cremation, the use of bodies for research and transplant, and the elimination of funeral services. Members of such societies are usually from professional occupations with high intellectual attainments. Yet research has indicated that this group is most anxious of three groups tested to avoid or disguise the presence of death.[4] As we will show in chapter 7, there may be good reasons for the practices that Fulton correlates with avoidance of the reality of death, but this depends on the meanings that one is enabled to see in the practices in the light of his faith.

Another form of denial of death is the accent on youth. Death is an infringement on keeping youthful in appearance, dress, and actions. The pretenses that both men and women use to appear younger than they are, from tinted hair to unsuitable clothes, deny the reality of aging. There is a differ-

---

[4] Fulton, ed., ibid., p. 103.

ence between youthful vigor and wise and healthful aging.[5] We usually trust our daughters with old men, unless they are trying to act younger than their age.

Verbally, most people will admit that death is a reality that must be accepted, provided one can get them to talk about death at all. The pressure comes at the unconscious level in forms of distraction: endless activities that satisfy the sensual and emotional demands of life, and sometimes the intellectual. However, the unwitting repression has a way of getting even with the body and mind, so that despair is the end result.[6]

Dumont and Foss suggest several reasons for the denial of death. It may arise out of the feeling of invulnerability that we had as children, which carries over into adult life. Furthermore, some of us believe that denying death has a magical effect, so that it won't happen to me, or at least not for a long time. Death also "contains overtones of personal failure and loss of status and identity." Death is so opposed to the life instinct that we cannot countenance it. Denial becomes the only way we can concentrate on the life we are now living.[7]

Continuous concentration on death, even in a pious manner as among some saints, is both morbid and paralyzing. Denial of death "is a healthier and more effective attitude for living life than is acceptance."[8] Yet this is no excuse for isolating the aging and dying from society. Retirement communities and nursing homes serve important functions, but they may have dangerous by-products, the chief of which is freedom from the shock of death of those who were once essential for our lives. The aging and dying are separated from society at a time when their numbers are increasing, and the expectation is that many of us will join them in the near future.

---

[5] Margaretta K. Bowers et al., *Counseling the Dying* (New York: Thomas Nelson & Sons, 1964), p. 71.
[6] Ignace Lepp, *Death and Its Mysteries* (New York: Macmillan, 1968), pp. 133–34.
[7] Dumont and Foss, *The American View of Death,* p. 45. Used by permission.
[8] Ibid.

ACCEPTANCE OF DEATH

Talcott Parsons has insisted, contrary to the evidence in the previous section, that American culture is moving toward the acceptance of death. The developing scientific orientation of the average man leads to the acceptance of death as normal and the denial of death as deviant. Modern medicine has led to a drastic reduction of death among infants and the young, so that death is seen as a natural concomitant of old age. As aging persons become a larger proportion of the population, we see ever more clearly that death is inevitable as the closing of life.[9]

Most people carry some form of life insurance, a large number have talked about their deaths with members of their family, and some people have provided wills and even made plans for their funerals. At least on the conscious level, there is an overt acceptance of death, but such studies fail to get at the depths of feelings and unwitting responses. Dumont and Foss think that the evidence about life insurance is to be taken seriously, for people do not spend a lot of money in preparation for something that might not happen.

We have mentioned euphemisms that disguise the fact of death, but there are others that are vivid and realistic: "he kicked the bucket," "he breathed his last," "he bit the dust," and "he went home feet first." Even on the screen and in books there is greater realism about death.

As we will show when looking at the research of Elisabeth Kübler-Ross in chapter 6, the terminally ill have a capacity not only to look squarely at death but to accept it.

Just as sex has come out into the open, so that books now contain more than we need to know, a plethora of books on death is coming. The subject is no longer on everyone's list of taboos and people are beginning to ask questions not only about death but also about any kind of afterlife.

---

[9] See ibid., pp. 53–54, based on Talcott Parsons, "Death in American Society: A Brief Working Paper," *American Behavioral Scientist* 6 (1963): 61–65.

Until new ground was broken by Herman Feifel in 1959, there was practically no scientific research into either the nature of death or attitudes toward death and dying. This change in attitude points toward an increasing acceptance of death as a natural attitude.

Our funeral practices may express both a denial and an acceptance of death. Many traditional ethnic practices, including wakes, sitting by the body, elaborate caskets, and ritualistic funeral services, are a way of honoring the dead. As Fulton says: "The funeral itself is a gift—both given and received by the deceased and by the survivors."[10] In some communities, all the relatives join in bearing the cost of an expensive funeral. The focus is on the death of someone who was loved. In some groups there is highly emotional grief, expressed in loud groaning and crying. Others, who come from cultures where understatement is traditional, control their manifestations of grief and may not work it out as well.

But there are some who have acted out new forms of response. They accept death but not all its rituals. They prefer cremation or giving bodies for medical research to burial, and may prefer to have their ashes spread (as the Hindus do) rather than buried. They may have a funeral or memorial service without the body present. They may choose a ritual that stresses the meaning of this life, grief over death, and trust in God rather than talk about the life to come. This approach offers the same opportunity for grief on the part of survivors, but lacks some of the specific imagery possible when the body is present. However, giving one's body or organs for transplant indicates an acceptance of death.

There are reasons to support the claim that many of us have an attitude of acceptance toward death. First, there is the rational attitude based on our scientific knowledge that death is inevitable, and that it is not necessarily associated

---

[10] Fulton, *Death and Identity*, p. 104. Used by permission.

with a painful process of dying. However, some who no longer fear death still fear certain diseases that may lead to death, such as cancer. Second, the mature person recognizes that he is finite and that all finite beings have a limit.[11] This enables us to take risks in our everyday living. Third, when one's life is fulfilled, especially after a normal span of years, death becomes the completion of that fulfillment. Last, death may be the lesser of two evils when one desperately desires relief from pain or frustration or meaninglessness in life.[12]

However, acceptance of death is not the same as reconciliation with death. Acceptance may be a kind of fatalism, so that one's will to live is blunted. We know a great deal today about psychosomatic medicine, and this leads to the conclusion that the attitude of the patient has much to do with his recovery from illness, even seemingly terminal ones. If one's will to live is blunted by resignation, the chances of recovery are lessened; whereas if there is strong assertion of the will to life (which is the positive side of the denial of death), remissions may occur.

There is a great difference, as Robert Fulton says, between being *prepared* to die and being *ready* to die. All that death education can do is help people be prepared, but one is never really ready until the time comes, and then much depends on his or her own faith and the meanings he or she has already discovered in this life.

ACCEPTANCE-DENIAL

There is a good deal of ambivalence about death. One may put it this way: "It depends on the days. Some of the things I read make me afraid, but others reassure me. Yes, all the same I think I'm afraid. In any case, the Gospels tell me that Christ was very much afraid of death. So I'm not surprised that I fear it too."[13]

[11] William E. Hocking, *Thoughts on Death and Life* (New York: Harper & Row, 1937), p. 20.
[12] See Dumont and Foss, *The American View of Death,* pp. 59–60.
[13] Quoted in André Godin, ed., *Death and Presence* (Brussels: Lumen Vitae Press, 1972), p. 43. Used by permission.

Research reveals this same ambiguity, partly because research projects have set out to study either denial or acceptance, but none has focused on both at the same time. Moreover, we keep coming upon interpretations of the same evidence as favorable to both sides, like funeral practices which seem to some to be a denial and to others to be an acceptance of death. And where the research has allowed for free responses, we often get acceptance and denial in the same paragraph. In one series of responses among unbelievers, four showed fear and six calm anticipation; among Protestants four indicated fear and two calm anticipation; and among Catholics it was five and three. Two unbelievers and one Catholic responded with rebellion or anger. It is too small a sample for any generalization, but it indicates the element of contradiction.[14]

People are often capable of showing opposite emotions. Children, whose emotions are easier to observe, may show hate and love toward parents in rapid succession. We may see a mixture of grief because of love and relief because of hate in the individual mourner. This points to Dumont and Foss's "acceptance-denial hypothesis," which is not fully supported by direct research but seems to be a hypothesis which future research should explore. That is, we both deny and accept death simultaneously.[15]

Attached to death are such positive meanings and connotations as deliverance from unbearable situations (for example, from pain, old age, or debt), undisturbed sleep and a state of complete rest, reunion with loved ones, rebirth (rejuvenation and reincarnation), love and sexuality, and an ultimate triumph over the uncertainties of life. Some of death's negative aspects include separation from cherished persons and things, loss (in many ways, such as loss of pleasures of the body), trauma (catastrophic or malevolent death), punishment, masochism, and mass destruction.[16]

14 Godin, ed., ibid., p. 42.
15 Dumont and Foss, *The American View of Death*, p. 95.
16 Ibid., p. 98.

Such conflict indicates that many of us do not know what to say in the face of death. How do we know where to get on the same wavelength with someone who may reflect any of a variety of the connotations of death? It not only leads to awkwardness when we have to talk to someone about to die or suffering grief, but it reduces us to silence in a conversation in which the topic of death comes up.

Those who have lost their previous confidence in religious teachings about life after death are sometimes reduced to anxiety because they no longer can count on anything beyond death. This may lead them from acceptance to denial, or from faith to fear and anxiety. But for some who have lived in fear of hell, the loss of belief may relieve them of this fear and free them to accept death as a natural event.

There is conflict between the life instinct and the death wish (if one accepts this Freudian hypothesis), or at least between zest for life and life that has lost its meaning. Even when life has lost its meaning, however, most people strive to continue to live; and when life is zestful, people fight against death. So the conflict remains. But it operates at an even deeper level. At the intellectual level, it is easy to recognize that death is inevitable and that there is no need to deny it, but at the emotional, unwitting, and unconscious level there is still a struggle. As Freud says: "The unconscious is immortal." "Reason and emotion conflict in this regard. That is, on a conscious, intellectual level the individual accepts his death, while on a generally unconscious, emotional plane he denies it."[17]

It is hard to imagine one's own death, except as an outsider, like Tom Sawyer appearing at his own funeral. "When I'm dead," says the child, "I will return and help Mommy cook breakfast." But since the "I" does the imagining and the "I" is what dies, there is no way to imagine one's own death. Death is a *total severance*, something intolerable to the unconscious. We can think of life as becoming and per-

---

[17] Ibid., p. 103.

ishing, but the perishing has a limit and the process stops.

At this dual level of intellect and emotions, we can get some evidence. When tests are conducted dealing with the intellect, there is acceptance of death, even when fear or dread is admitted. When the tests are aimed at uncovering emotional responses, they bring out denial. Arnold Toynbee recounts the story of

one believer who was intensely afraid of the prospect of death, though he was conscious of having lived righteously in the main and though he was utterly confident that he was one hundred per cent correct in his theological tenets. Logically, he ought to have felt assured that, after death, he could not only go to heaven but would be received there as a V.I.P. All the same, he was unable to face the prospect of death with equanimity.[18]

For many people, the issue is not this divided or conflicting because they are not conflicted themselves. From time to time, they may say that death is an unpleasant thought when it intrudes, but they accept it as inevitable no matter what the afterlife may be. They are like Bernard, the farmer of whom Ignace Lepp writes, who thought that maybe people like Camus and Sartre were a little crazy if they thought that life is meaningless. Bernard finds meaning in working his farm and living with his wife and children. He assists his elderly parents and takes part in community life. Bernard is in love with life and hopes to live a long time. But, he says, "We can die in peace when we have done our duty." Here is a simple, balanced attitude that is highly to be desired.[19]

Death is an end and therefore a threat to our future, but to deny or accept it is really not the main issue, for we need to know how to value the present. This can lead us to a realistic view of death.

---

[18] Arnold Toynbee et al., *Man's Concern with Death* (London: Hodder & Stoughton, 1968), pp. 93–94. Used by permission of McGraw-Hill.
[19] Lepp, *Death and Its Mysteries,* p. 138. Used by permission.

CHAPTER FIVE

A Realistic View
of Death

In 1931, George Albert Coe wrote an essay with the title "A Realistic View of Death."[1] By using the term realistic Coe was insisting not only on taking facts seriously but on accepting an ethical realism as well. Unless we can fit death into our view of the good life, we have not solved the problem. Coe believed that good and evil were terms with meaning for our lives, and he sought to include death within the meaning of life. His realism enabled him to see religion experimentally in two ways:

Through the active testing of hypotheses we increase our foresight and control, and at the same time we learn whether what is deepest in us can cooperate with the more-than-us that has us in its power. If it can, then here is the basic fact of what religion calls fellowship with God.[2]

Some would respond to this by saying that a realistic attitude toward death is "accepting the inevitable." The Stoics did this, because they saw the universe as rational and good, but they placed the emphasis on a natural life that did not

---

[1] Douglas C. Macintosh, ed., *Religious Realism* (New York: Macmillan, 1931), pp. 179–91. Used by permission.
[2] Ibid., p. 182.

include the process of dying. There was a Stoic passivity about death that has a heroic quality about it, but the emphasis was on resignation rather than reconciliation. For some of us, this is as far as we can go, but it does not see death as having value.

On the other side, the Christian view has traditionally interpreted death as an enemy, as something unnatural. One way to escape the "wages of sin" is through repentance. There is a sense in which death is transcended in this life, for there can be forgiveness and a restoration of the self to a right relation with God. Furthermore, there is the promise of resurrection or immortality as a way around death. The hope of resurrection unto eternal life is a compelling and helpful doctrine, but it does not resolve Coe's major problem, "for, whatever its truth or error, it does not assign any ethical significance whatever to the experience of dying."[3]

Coe's claim is that death has value; it is good that death is; without death we would be in a bad way. Yet in the modern search for meaning, dying is often reduced to an experience of nothingness: it is seen as due to chance or accident or the capricious will of God. It "is losing its old meanings without acquiring new ones."[4] So we need to look hard at the experience of dying and death in terms of our judgments about good and evil.

THE VALUE OF DEATH

Death may be interpreted as a palliative. It is a positive release from many kinds of evil or pain or suffering or unbearable burdens. There are human organisms which are wracked with pain to whom death is a welcome release. There are others who have suffered such mental decay or damage that their distinctive humanness has already vanished. Many people who can no longer stand to live will ask for a prayer that they might die, or will request that the

---

[3] Ibid., p. 181.
[4] Ibid.

doctor discontinue his heroic efforts to keep them alive, or will resort to suicide. Death is capable of moderating evil.

From middle age onward life takes a downward curve. It is not surprising that most professional athletes are forced to retire between the ages of thirty-three and forty, and only a rarely gifted athlete can continue beyond that age. One's physical powers decline, including sexual potency and the capacity for heavy work. There are benefits of old age, such as increased wisdom and openness to new experiences, and there are many other assets that make the aged an asset to society—an asset that is not widely used today. Sooner or later, however, whether the values contributed by the aging are utilized by society or not, there comes a time when the aged are a liability; they get in the way of the imagination and vigor of younger people; they become dependent on society; and sooner or later they can contribute only one value: they can get out of the way by dying. Death, then, becomes a positive value.

This aging process is not necessarily chronological. Many people become useless long before they have reached three score and ten years, and others are making contributions as they approach the century mark. Plato wrote his *Laws* at about the age of eighty. In some fields, especially when it includes mental activity, men and women may achieve latter-day fame like Grandma Moses. But normally there is a decline in mental plasticity, leading to unimaginative and sluggish leadership by older people and to frustration by the young. As Coe bluntly states: "Aggressive minds are thankful, and properly so, when reactionary old men are rendered powerless by being removed from the scene."[5]

The death of the old is the gift of life to the young. Whenever the birth rate gets out of balance with the death rate, we are in trouble. In modern culture, advances in medical care have increased the chances of infant survival and of extended life at the same time, thus leading to almost impos-

---

[5] Ibid., p. 185.

sible efforts to restore a proper balance by lowering the birth rate. Nature, when not interfered with by man, has ways of keeping generations and species in balance. But once the ecology is disturbed, we may have both overpopulation and underpopulation, so that while we are fighting to save certain species in danger of extinction we are at the same time struggling to keep down the population of elephants in game parks because of overgrazing. If there were no natural death, we could no longer remain human, for we would be forced to kill off the aged in order to make room for new populations.

The generation gap is bad enough as it is, but without death we would have gaps as great as between the Stone Age people and the astronauts. The prudence and rigidity of the old need to give way to the imprudence and flexibility of the young, and the democracy of death makes that possible. No one is indispensable, and death keeps reminding us of that fact.[6]

One way of looking at the problem is to ask what would happen if there were no death. Donald P. Irish provides a statement by a student:

The elimination of death would bring about many changes. First of all, it would mean a huge population explosion. New ways of supporting more people would have to be found immediately. This would probably be the main concern of technology. If people knew they were going to live forever, they wouldn't need to worry so much about getting ahead. They would have more time to reach their goals. Social processes would slow down. The nuclear family could remain a stable unit longer, marriage could take place later, and in every way there'd be less press for time. It would be harder for society to change. Traditions would still be there in the older people, who would outnumber the younger. Society could become stagnant. The world would be united against the problems of too many people.

---

[6] See William W. Hocking, *Thoughts on Death and Life* (New York: Harper & Row, 1937), pp. 13–15.

More people would mean less primary group relationships. Formal control would take precedence. This would mean stricter government. . . . It would be impossible to provide food, shelter, jobs and education to an ever-increasing number of people. People would be unsatisfied and restless.

Nearly everything man now knows would be interrupted by the elimination of death. New values and social pressures would develop. People would react differently, in groups and alone.

Politics would be concerned with control, economics with support, and religion would be earth-centered. If death were eliminated, there would be no reason for a religious belief in life eternal after death and the hope that after death we would be rewarded.[7]

A realistic view of death sees it as a natural rather than an unnatural event.[8] Many theologians have looked upon death as unnatural, blaming it on Adam or on man's sin. For them death is an enemy. The *new* religious view is that death is both natural and good; it is necessary so that values can continue in this world; it is the only basic possibility for the development of mankind.

Death is also personal. It is highly individualized, so that no man can do your dying for you. There is a sense in which Jesus Christ died for man's sins, but this does not eliminate the need for our own death. Death is destructive in that it means the cessation of one's earthly existence, but it is also an event of creative and responsible selfhood. It means that life has a time limit, that we are finite, and therefore our lives can have shape and character. Life without structure and limit can have no purpose, and therefore it loses its meaning. What identifies one as a human being is that one exists for a certain length of time, and within that time span he establishes the meaning of his life, the values to which

[7] Quoted in Donald P. Irish, *Death Education,* ed. Betty R. Green and Donald P. Irish (Cambridge, Mass.: Schenkman, 1971), p. 61. Used by permission.

[8] See Richard W. Doss, "Towards a Theology of Death," *Pastoral Psychology* 23 (June 1972): 15–23.

he adheres, and his contribution to the future. This recognition of *limit* means that one has self-knowledge and therefore is enabled to accept death as good even if he is not yet personally reconciled to death.[9]

One believer put it this way:

Death is all part of life itself. Human life is a life that doesn't go on indefinitely, a life that will end. I'm convinced that one must accept the fact of growing old, of dying eventually. Death is all part of life itself and if man were immortal, life would be meaningless. Our life has an exceptional meaning because our days are numbered.[10]

Death is also social. The only way a human being becomes a person is through relationships with others, and therefore he finds his values within the social process. Death is a way of becoming absent from a community and therefore it disrupts the life of the community. Death not only is a natural event affecting the body and an individual or personal event affecting consciousness but is also a social event affecting the community of the living. We are dependent on community in the becoming and perishing, the living and dying which marks our share in time. It is because we live in community that we find the secret of the meaning of human life, which is love. Death means the destruction of those relationships of love, even though there is a sense in which love transcends death for those still living. Because we see death as a threat to the continuation of the relationships of love, we are anxious about death at this level even when we have acquired a positive attitude toward death at the natural and personal level.

But community is not always the expression of love. We live through many battles and struggles in community, and we acquire many burdens, some of which may be irrational

---

[9] See Hocking, *Thoughts on Death and Life*, pp. 15, 19.
[10] Cited in André Godin, ed., *Death and Presence* (Brussels: Lumen Vitae Press, 1972), p. 44. Used by permission.

and others which are filled with hate. As Hocking says: "*This* self, scarred, marked, identified, dated, need not live forever,"[11] for death can mean freedom from such excess baggage.

Death is also mystery. Perhaps this is why there is little literature on death and great literature on life after death. Although the Jewish Bible does not speak at length about death except to be realistic about it, the influence of Zoroastrianism, which taught resurrection after death, affected both later Judaism and Christianity. Death is a mystery because no one has absolute certainty about what happens after death.

But death remains a mystery also because no man can imagine himself as dead. We even contemplate our own death from the outside, as those who are still living. We can grasp the concept of the process of dying but not the end of the process. This is why we can speak of death as a mystery and also why we can remain open to the hope that beyond death there may be another form of existence, but hoping is not knowing.

Finally, death is fulfillment. One lives his life and at the end finds that it has been good. Because life has a limit, he has discovered that within those limits of time and finitude, he has tasted deeply of the meaning of life. There has been no endless time to squander, but only this time in which to live. How he has filled this time is what matters, for time has provided the structure for his life.

EARLY DEATH

It is all very well to speak of death as fulfillment or of the values of death for the aged or even for the necessity of death to make room for new generations on an earth threatened with overpopulation, but this does not provide us with a realistic answer to the problem of death at an early age.

Coe faced up to this problem. Early death eliminates the

---

[11] Hocking, *Thoughts on Death and Life.* pp. 23–24. Used by permission.

value of death as a palliative, he says, and it frustrates the
kinds of value built up through a longer life. Is this not a
tearing of the ethical fabric of our view? But where do we
draw the line? As Coe writes,

When steady objectivity and a long perspective become possible,
how often do we perceive that the lost worker or leader had
already accomplished his distinctive task, had made himself indispensable. Further, the loss of a significant man often makes
his meaning more clear and convincing than further life could
have made it.[12]

But is this realism or romanticism? We can point to many
who have died after accomplishing much, a Joan of Arc or
Martin Luther King or Mozart, but does the quality of their
accomplishments depend on the shortness of their lives? A
choice of death as a means to a goal, whether it be Jesus at
midlife or Socrates in old age, does not depend on one's age.
What potential for good was eliminated by these early
deaths?

It may be, however, that Coe is right in those cases in
which death highlights what a person stood for, and this
may assist in bringing about the good that he stood for. I
suppose one could argue that John Kennedy's death made
possible legislation for civil rights, but we do not know
whether those same bills would have been passed had he
lived. But early death by martyrdom is only one side of the
argument, and even if accepted does not take care of those
who die a premature natural death for no moral reason. We
will have to dig more deeply into theological issues to resolve
this problem, and will turn to it in chapters 8 and 10.

The issue gets even sharper when the very young die.
Here is the situation of obviously unfulfilled potentialities.
Coe admits this, and can only say that "the quality of one's
living" can "reduce one's vulnerability to the shafts of the

---

[12] Coe, "A Realistic View of Death," ed. Macintosh, *Religious Realism*, p. 187.

Destroyer."[13] We do say no to death when it happens so early, and it is difficult to provide even a "qualified 'Yes.'" He finds here a distinction between the "will to live" and the "will to love" by which a more positive attitude will develop.

Children and young people do face death with courage and equanimity, and this is always a personal victory for them. Coe tells the story of a young teacher who had a fatal malady, yet she was able to cheer her friends who commiserated with her. She explained:

From childhood I was never able to be religious in the same way as people about me. I couldn't pray as they did; it seemed unreal. But when I saw one of the tots in my kindergarten take a difficult step toward a fine personality, there, to me, was prayer; and when I saw one of my university students struggle with a point and finally master it, again this was prayer.[14]

In this kind of ethical creativity, she saw her religious faith in action, and, as she said, she just "faced the whole situation," which included her forthcoming painful death.

This approach puts death in perspective. The problem is to find something or someone worth living for. This is a matter of choice over a lifetime, and there are many people whose lives suffer from meaninglessness because of either free or forced choices of career, marriage, or friends. But we are helped to find what meaning is actually there if we place ourselves in a perspective about the nature of the universe in which life is a gift to be realized. Then the emphasis is not on length of life or time of death but on the meanings to be expressed in whatever life we have. There are many persons who "are willing to sell their souls, their bodies and their honor for a few more years of life," and yet "they have

---

[13] Ibid., p. 188.
[14] Ibid., p. 189.

no idea how life should be lived."[15] Because death is a reality, we have to place a value on the time we have.

INDIVIDUAL RESPONSES

All that we have said so far about attitudes toward death needs to be qualified by the fact that it is an individual who dies, and he has specific beliefs and attitudes which are peculiarly his own. The individual may fit into one or more groups that are on the side of either the fear or the acceptance of death. There is probably a continuum running from complete denial to complete acceptance, with most people somewhere near the middle.

Because we have little guidance about the nature of death when we are young, and because much of what we feel about death depends on the happenstance of being included in or excluded from experiences of death, or even of having no opportunity to observe death at all, we may have a background that is hard to identify. Many children hear more about the afterlife than they do about death, so that the reality of death as the end escapes their attention, although they may be taught about Jesus' crucifixion and resurrection, or may be told that Aunt Susie is with Jesus or has gone to heaven.

Whether one believes strongly in the afterlife as an adult may affect one's attitude. In some cases, as we have indicated, belief in immortality serves as a denial of death because the soul automatically enters heaven. In other cases, death is dealt with in a mature way, with the expectation that one commits himself to God for whatever existence there may be after death, but death is still an event to be faced realistically.

There is some evidence that women are more likely than men to think about death and to express a death wish. Women are more likely to accept a religious interpretation

---

[15] Ignace Lepp, *Death and Its Mysteries* (New York: Macmillan, 1968), p. 149. Used by permission.

of death and immortality. They identify their death fears during experiences such as sexual maturation, menstruation, childbirth, and menopause. Some women fear the loss of physical beauty in a culture that values youthful appearance. Women, probably because they outlive men, are more likely to fear the death of others more than their own. Men, on the other hand, associate death with violence more often.[16]

Among some elderly people there is a loss of the fear of death, but no denial in most cases. They know they have fulfilled all the goals that are possible for them, even when they are dissatisfied with their accomplishments. This, however, does not eliminate negative reactions to death. As they move into a state of terminal illness, they still go through the same process of dying as younger people.

Dumont and Foss suggest that there is a subjective time factor that affects one's expectations about death. If time seems to go rapidly, death may seem nearer, even though the actual time may be the same for two people. To one death may seem close at seventy and to another it may seem far off. Early retirement may affect this, for when one has nothing to do with his time he may seem to be moving toward death at a more rapid rate than a person who is fully occupied.[17]

There are some who have a greater fear of accidents, which may or may not be based on statistical evidence concerning the risks involved. The fear of flying is a good example, for getting to the airport is actually more dangerous. There is little correlation between the risks we take and actual danger. More often we fear the deaths of others due to accidents. Parents worry, often unduly, about their children who are out late in automobiles or on motorcycles; wives worry about husbands who are late arriving home. We often fear the worst simply because we do not know what has caused a change in plans.

---

[16] Richard G. Dumont and Dennis C. Foss, *The American View of Death: Acceptance or Denial?* (Cambridge, Mass.: Schenkman, 1972), p. 87.
[17] Ibid., pp. 90–91.

APPROPRIATE DEATH

A realistic view of death should contain the concept of a wholesome or appropriate death.[18] It is appropriate, as a reflection of a way of life, for a captain to go down with his ship, or for a Socrates to drink the hemlock, or for a Jesus to be crucified. There are others, such as Christians who risk charges of heresy, leaders who risk assassination, or those who risk death in the line of duty, such as policemen, firemen, and soldiers and sailors and airmen. But how does the average person who shares none of these opportunities die a wholesome or appropriate death?

Weisman and Hackett suggest four principle requirements: "(1) conflict is reduced; (2) compatibility with the ego ideal is achieved; (3) continuity of important relationships is preserved or restored; (4) consummation of a wish is brought about."[19] This leads to a kind of maturity in the face of death that is appropriate. Herman Feifel suggests several other factors not within the patient's control, such as

(1) psychological maturity, . . . (2) the kind of coping techniques available to him, (3) variables of religious orientation, age, sociometric status, etc., (4) severity of the organic process, and (5) the attitudes of the physician and other significant persons in the patient's world.[20]

In short, if we are mature in facing death and if we are also fortunate in having the kind of care that assists us in coping with it, we may have an appropriate end. But there is still the process of dying to go through, and this is not easy, involving us in attitudes of denial, anger, depression, acceptance, and hope.

---

[18] A. D. Weisman and T. P. Hackett, "The Treatment of the Dying," *Current Psychiatric Therapies,* ed. J. H. Musserman (New York: Grune & Stratton, 1962), cited in Margaretta K. Bowers et al., *Counseling the Dying* (New York: Thomas Nelson & Sons, 1964), p. 48.

[19] A. D. Weisman and T. P. Hackett, "Predilection to Death," *Psychosomatic Medicine* 23 (1961): 232–56, cited in Bowers et al., *Counseling the Dying,* p. 50.

[20] Herman Feifel, ed., *The Meaning of Death* (New York: McGraw-Hill, 1959), p. 126. Used by permission.

CHAPTER SIX

When Death Is Certain

Death education comes too late if it is postponed until death is expected, for it is like delaying sex education until a couple is in the marriage bed. We need to have an understanding of the process of dying and the necessity of death long before our last illness. Belief in one's own death is acquired and usually comes late in life, although an awareness that one must die is somewhere in the unconscious after about the age of six. To be alive means to have a past and a future, both of which contribute to the meaning of the present.

Sooner or later we come to the belief that we will die, and finally to the point where death is certain sometime in the near future. We face a crisis. We become dimly aware that we might die, but we may not have accurate information, and this may be difficult to get.

There is an increasing tendency to tell the dying patient the truth, partly because people have more medical knowledge than in the past. Doctors have discovered that most patients can handle the truth and behave better when they know what to expect. It is also becoming clear that death is much more than a biological event, with psychological, ethical, social, and religious meanings.

When the patient knows what his prognosis is, communication opens up not only between doctor and patient but between patient and nurses, family, friends, and chaplain. The result may be an improvement in the patient's condition, but it may also lead one into a series of protective devices such as denial or anger or depression. If the patient rejects the information, the doctor does no good by insisting that the truth must be recognized.

There are hazards in telling the patient he or she will die. The obvious one is that there may be a remission that no one expects on medical grounds. This may destroy faith in the doctor or in God. He may be told in a blunt or heartless way, without adequate preparation. Sometimes the truth leads to a hopelessness that stops all meaningful activity, and it may take good counseling to assist the patient to continue to plan for his family and children, or for his friends or his business.

Because dying is such a lonely experience, telling the truth tends to keep open the lines of communication and therefore of the sense of community. But the manner in which the patient is told becomes important here, and each patient will accept the truth in a different way. It is not necessary to say that within the week or month you will be dead, but you can be told that a cure is impossible although there is hope for some improvement.

Another factor in preparation for death is the religion of the patient. It is important for a Roman Catholic to be told, so that he can establish that he is in a sanctifying relationship with God and has access to a priest. For the Jewish patient, his well-being is paramount, and if he is to die in peace he ought to have time to prepare for it, although compassion is essential to the relationship. There should be time for repentance. Protestants desire to get their own house in order, sometimes to have time for prayer and Bible reading, and certainly to be ministered to by family, friends, and a pastor.[1]

The physician is the key person at this point, for he needs to use both personal and professional resources to assist the patient face death in such a way that he will remain fully human. His slogan, as Gardner Murphy says, is: "Don't let hope die, but don't minimize the gravity of the situation."[2]

RESPONSES TO DYING

"The great bulk of normal men who face death are terrified, and they have all sorts of different ways of controlling it— not always successfully, but some kind of coping techniques."[3]

If the process of dying begins with an emergency, there is the flying trip to the hospital in a siren-screeching ambulance, followed by being exposed to all kinds of technology in the emergency room, often without any communication. It becomes an impersonal process leading to even more of the same if the patient survives long enough to be admitted to the hospital. If the patient is terminally ill, he may not be given any information and so is left with his own imagination running wild, allowing his fears to build up.

But perhaps along the way he comes to the realization that he is going to die, or he has been told by the physician that his chances of recovery are practically nil. As Carlozzi says, "a person, even in the face of death, tends to remain true to his basic personality structure."[4] Yet one has to learn to die, for, Weisman writes, "while we can readily

---

[1] See Margaretta K. Bowers et al., *Counseling the Dying* (New York: Thomas Nelson & Sons, 1964), pp. 99–110; Samuel Stoddard and Helmuth Nathan, eds., *Should the Patient Know the Truth?* (New York: Springer, 1955).

[2] Gardner Murphy, *The Meaning of Death,* ed. Herman Feifel (New York: McGraw-Hill, 1959), p. 330. Used by permission.

[3] Ibid., p. 336.

[4] Carl G. Carlozzi, *Death and Contemporary Man* (Grand Rapids: Eerdmans, 1968), p. 31.

claim that dying is a process that is as fully complicated as living, because it *is* a part of living, to say that people die as they have lived is from a psychological viewpoint wholly meaningless."[5] There may be some personality changes that are wholly unpredictable, not necessarily connected with the organic condition. In an age of mass man and technology, dying remains a highly individualized process on which the patient imposes his own traits.

REPORTS FROM THE DYING

We are beginning to understand what dying patients go through. Against much opposition from doctors and staff, Elisabeth Kübler-Ross has established seminars to study the dying, based on interviews with patients who are incurably ill or in danger of dying. These seminars are conducted so that medical students and others can observe, and out of the results of these interviews Dr. Ross has established the five steps through which many patients go: denial, anger, bargaining, depression, and acceptance, with hope in the background at every level.

There is nothing automatic about these five steps, however, for it is clear that not every person goes through all the stages in that order and many die before what might be called the "death work" is finished.[6] But the stages do serve as possible moves through which a dying person may go, and they are not normally reversible.

It was not easy to set up the seminars. When Dr. Ross finally found a patient who was willing to be interviewed, the patient was enthusiastic. So Dr. Ross promised to return the next day, although the patient wanted to talk right then. Tomorrow turned out to be too late, as the patient was unable to be interviewed and died a few hours later.

Most of the patients interviewed were not near death in

---

[5] Avery D. Weisman, *On Dying and Denying* (New York: Behavioral Publications, 1972), p. 122. Used by permission.
[6] See Philip A. Anderson, "Death and Dying," *Religion and Society*, XVIII, 2 (June 1971), p. 48.

the immediate sense. Some of them had remissions and returned home for a time; others remained in the hospital for a long period. But all of them had been diagnosed as having a potentially fatal illness and had begun to come to terms with the fact. When they were still strong enough to think things through and to make intelligent plans about finances and family responsibilities was a good time for the dying to become teachers to the medical students, nurses, doctors, and chaplains who took part in the seminars.

DENIAL

The first response to the information that one has but a short time to live is denial: "Who me?" There may be withdrawal from further conversation as the patient struggles with the bad news. He may ignore the symptoms of his illness. He may begin talking about irrelevant matters or turn to views of life after death or daydream.[7]

Of course, denial may begin earlier. There is a great deal of denial of old age until inability to perform, illness, or the rules of society force one to admit the facts. There are many ways in which people deny that they are not what they used to be. Sometimes this experience may come from being expendable on the labor market due to changes in technology. "The old does not give way to the new; the new invariably thrusts the old aside. Only in tribal life and in early traditions do the very old have a distinct place in society. Even then, it may be just a myth constructed over another myth."[8]

Weisman sees denial operating at three levels. First-order denial refers to the patient's perception of his illness; second-order denial has to do with the inferences drawn by the patient about the implications of his illness. Third-order denial refers to death itself.[9] The latter seldom occurs until

---

[7] Elisabeth Kübler-Ross, *On Death and Dying* (New York: Macmillan, 1969), pp. 41–42.
[8] Weisman, *On Dying and Denying,* p. 139.
[9] Ibid., p. 67.

the terminal stage is reached, and not always then, for the patient may skip this step.

Denial is a good protective device. It may keep the doctor from giving information, for he readily sees that the patient is not ready. A period of denial may help the patient get ready for the next step. Rollin J. Fairbanks writes: "Each human being has the inalienable right to deny his dying if he so desires."[10]

Much of Dr. Ross's book consists of case studies which are difficult to summarize. They show ways in which the various attitudes toward death are expressed. One patient denied that she had a fatal illness and went to a faith healer, who assured her that she was perfectly all right. When she was brought back to the hospital she wanted to show the doctors that God had cured her. She became an unruly patient who did not follow her diet and showed symptoms that combined denial with suicidal tendencies, like overeating. Finally, after a period of confusion covering several weeks, one day she said to the psychiatrist, "You have such warm hands. I hope you are going to be with me when I get colder and colder." She had moved from denial to acceptance.[11]

ANGER

Denial cannot be maintained for very long. As realization comes that one is in the process of dying, the next step may be anger, resentment, envy, rage: "Why couldn't it have been some useless old codger instead of me?" Because the anger has no specific object except death itself, which is hard to personalize, it is spread in all directions, making it difficult for the hospital staff to cope with it. The anger strikes at unanticipated times and objects. Everything is always wrong, and nothing that is done makes it any better.

No matter when we die, we are likely to think of death as

---

[10] Rollin J. Fairbanks, *Journal of Pastoral Care,* LVIII, (Summer 1964), p. 96.
[11] Kübler-Ross, *On Death and Dying,* p. 45. Copyright © 1969 by Elisabeth Kübler-Ross. Used by permission of Macmillan Publishing Co., Inc.

premature. Think of all the plans that are interrupted. One person may have been working to establish a new company, and he won't live long enough to see it functioning; another may have been saving for a romanticized retirement in some Shangri La, and now this expectation is canceled; another has been waiting until the time when he could start a new hobby or read poetry or go traveling. No wonder dying people get angry and stay that way.

Some people are carrying over anger that began in childhood, and of course they are unable to meet a situation beyond their control without anger. Others, who may have operated in life without undue anger, find they cannot handle their feelings in the face of death. They express their anger toward doctors who cannot guarantee continued life, at God who is taking them away from this life, or at the care being received in the hospital. Because the staff members do not always realize that the anger is not directed at them but that they are caught in the unaimed anger of the patient, they often respond with anger or avoidance, which only increases the anger of the patient.

When such patients are allowed to express their feelings without being judged, they usually move on to another stage in their development.

BARGAINING

Many patients have been angry at God for cutting their lives short, and he has not responded to their anger. So now they have another approach: bargaining with God. "If I am cured, I will go to church every Sunday for the rest of my life." Like little children, they will be good if Santa Claus will come. Sometimes they will bargain for just a few more days—and then a few more.

One patient was in great pain and wished to attend her son's wedding. Writes Dr. Ross:

With combined efforts, we were able to teach her self-hypnosis which enabled her to be quite comfortable for several hours. She had made all sorts of promises if she could only live long enough to attend this marriage. The day preceding the wedding she left the hospital as an elegant lady. Nobody would have believed her real condition. She was "the happiest person in the whole world" and looked radiant. I wondered what her reaction would be when the time was up for which she had bargained.

I will never forget the moment when she returned to the hospital. She looked tired and somewhat exhausted and—before I could say hello—said, "Now don't forget I have another son!"[12]

No matter what the bargain, the patients always want one round more.

Most bargains are with God, with the promise being to dedicate one's life to him. But occasionally the patient seeks to make a bargain with the doctor: "Keep me alive one more week (month, year) and I will donate my organs or my body to science." In some cases there may be guilt feelings behind such bargains, and if so a chaplain might well seek to identify them and work with them.

This kind of bargaining can get in the way of a healthy approach to dying, for when we deal with forces that we cannot control we are using escapist magical thinking in place of coming to grips with reality.[13] This belief in magic often turns one to various kinds of faith healers, and when that fails there is a return to denial and despair.

DEPRESSION

Once denial of dying becomes impossible, the patient may go into a depression. First of all there is a sense of loss in reaction to the news. The removal of a breast or uterus may say to a woman that she is no longer feminine, although most women are as good sexually afterward as before, and sometimes better. The cost of hospital care may point to financial burdens that will mean the loss of college education to children or force a mother into the work force while

---

[12] Ibid., p. 83.
[13] Bowers et al., *Counseling the Dying*, p. 145.

children are small. There is the loss of many hopes and plans which now cannot be carried out. For many, it is even too late for a last fling.

But there is also depression in preparation for death, for death is an occasion for grief on the part of the dying. One does not tell a grieving person that he should not grieve at the death of a family member. So also we should recognize that grief on the part of a dying person is part of his preparation for death. If he can work on and work out his grief, he will move in a more healthy way to the acceptance of death.

Death is a departure from all whom one loves. It is a giving up of spouse, children, friends all at once. When we are left behind, we grieve at the loss of one person; when we die, we grieve at the loss of all persons who mean anything to us. We may have some satisfaction in what we have meant to them, but we no longer have a personal relationship with them. We are isolated and alone in our dying, and at the end we have none of them.

This is the grief that needs to be worked through during the period of depression. Each time a person leaves the sickroom, the patient may think that this is the last time he will see him. So the process of dying becomes grief at the last visit of many people, and at death there is no consciousness of any person around one.

Just as we learn to handle our grief when we are survivors, so we need to handle our grief when we are dying. But it takes survivors a long time after death to work out their grief, while the dying person has only the time between the realization that he will die until death, and this may be a very short time. No wonder there is depression.

Religious faith may be helpful here, in that we believe that God is love and that we find our meaning in life and death through our trust in him. If we are accepted as we are by God, whether living or dying, then we can commit ourselves to him as we commit those whom we love to him. For many, this is enough. For others, there is another step to

believe in some kind of reunion in a new life in God's kingdom. At any rate, God is at work to help us overcome our
grief, and from grief we can move to acceptance.

ACCEPTANCE

When we speak of an attitude of acceptance of death as it
approaches, we do not mean that it is welcomed with any
kind of enthusiasm. It is a passive stage after the struggle
is over. This is why death seems so peaceful, for the pain,
the agonized striving, the anticipation of a tomorrow are
gone. It is a peace of diminishing interest, with shorter
visits and fewer visitors, with little verbal communication,
with periods of silence, and with the need for occasional
reassurance that someone significant to the dying is present.

With the very old, this peacefulness is often buttressed
with a kind of absentmindedness and forgetfulness, which
may include flashbacks to events of many years before.
They hardly seem aware of the present, yet in lucid moments
they may speak of their impending death. They may know
they are surrounded by loving family and friends, and
yet they may seem indifferent. But we know that many dying
persons who cannot communicate are often very much aware
of everything that is said to them. At the very end they may
spend some time in a coma, when there is no understanding
(as far as we can tell), and then they seem simply to slip
away.

But young people move into an attitude of acceptance,
too. Many times their concern is for those who are being
left behind, worrying about parents or wives or husbands
and young children, and recognizing that death at this time
is a tragedy for all concerned. We see this acceptance, which
is other than fatalism, among young victims of accidents
and wars as well as among young people who have fatal illnesses. They have moved from resentment to acceptance,
even though there is little time to contemplate such things
when death is quick.

Acceptance of death sometimes is more positive among

those with a strong belief in immortality, and especially those with a conviction that they are right with the Lord and will see him soon. As long as they are able, they continue to read the Bible and to have prayers or Holy Communion, for these activities serve to reinforce their conviction that they are going to pass from this life to a heavenly one. Others with equally strong religious convictions may not have any guarantee of life after death, but see religious practices as strengthening their acceptance of death as an end, no matter what the future may hold.

Acceptance, which is different from fatalism because it is laced with hope—hope sometimes of recovery, sometimes of life after death, sometimes of facing death as a reality—is dynamic and positive even though it moves quickly toward a peaceful resignation and sense of reconciliation, a reversal of the birth experience as one goes from life to death rather than from birth to life.

HOPE

No matter how accepting of death a patient may be, there is always an element of hope for the continuation of life. This is not the Christian hope of life after death, which may also be present, but simply a hope that death may be postponed, that the time is not yet, that there will be a remission, that medical science will come up with a miracle cure. Patients seem to do better when doctors allow them to have this hope. When patients lose hope, they usually die very quickly. The experience of being interviewed on how they feel about death may lead to a degree of remission. They lose hope because they are isolated and out of communication, and the conversation brings them back into the human community. About half of them are discharged to go home or to a nursing home and come back later in most cases to die.

There are cures that seem to be miracles. The story is told of an old man who was isolated and lonely in the hospital. No one could reach him through any kind of communication. It appeared that he was dying from cancer. A little boy wandered into the hospital, and for some reason no one stopped him. He found the old man, who turned out to be his grandfather. From that day on, the old man began to recover, and in a few weeks he left the hospital with no sign of his malignancy. There is an emotional base to some kinds of illness, even when the symptoms are physical, about which we have very little understanding, but such factors may account for remarkable and seemingly miraculous remissions. So we never give up hope.

We said at the beginning of this book that many people have no direct experience of the death of others, which is one way to come to an understanding of the death that comes to all of us. The clergyman who ministers to a dying person often does so in silence. He learns that the moment of death is not frightening or painful, in spite of talk about the agony of death. What the clergyman becomes aware of is that this unique person, who has persisted through a process of becoming and perishing, is about to disappear after living out his limit, and that he leaves behind his own gifts to mankind, whether they be minor or major, for this is what he has been.

Those who have the strength and the love to sit with a dying patient in the *silence that goes beyond words* will know that this moment is neither frightening nor painful, but a peaceful cessation of the functioning of the body. Watching a peaceful death of a human being reminds us of a falling star; one of the million lights in a vast sky that flares up for a brief moment only to disappear into the endless night forever. To be a therapist to a dying patient makes us aware of the uniqueness of each individual in this vast sea of humanity. It makes us aware of our finiteness, our limited lifespan. Few of us live beyond our three score and ten years and yet in that brief time most of us create and live a unique biography and weave ourselves into the fabric of human history.[14]

---

[14] Kübler-Ross, *On Death and Dying*, p. 276.

CHAPTER SEVEN

Dying with Dignity

A very Weisman speaks of an ideal prototype for dying, in which the patient receives medical attention promptly and receives a correct diagnosis, thus establishing a confident and compassionate relationship with the doctor. Then as the disease is extended he will begin to give up his control of his life and delegate counter-controls to others, confident that his dignity will not be compromised. He makes his own choices as the process of dying goes on and accepts death as a fully human person.

Of course, there is no such ideal for most of us. Sooner or later that inevitable end will come, with no more regressions or reversible symptoms. But sometimes the physician moves too soon or too late, and proper timing is essential for the transfer of controls.[1]

If our development as persons has been fortunate and we have achieved a degree of maturity in living through our relationships with other persons, death comes into the picture to sharpen our focus. Writes Brantner:

Here death makes its greatest gift, for the sure and ever-present awareness that I shall die much sooner than I would wish, and that others are moving as quickly and surely to the same end,

---

[1] See Avery D. Weisman, *On Dying and Denying* (New York: Behavioral Publications, 1972), pp. 119–21.

enhances all human relationships from that of casual acquaintance to that of deepest love. . . . If only we can learn to act as if we are going to die then death loses much of its power over us. . . . If we realize that love is stronger than death, we may see that length of life is not important.[2]

Again, this is an idealized portrait. We still want to live to the fullness of our days. Love helps us to see meaning in continuing relationships, and it assists us when we are facing death and especially during the process of dying. Death puts love in proper perspective, so that we can live in love as if each day may be our last one. But the poignancy of death is such that we are not really brave.

It helps to go through what Weisman calls death rehearsal.[3] We can do this at any time, for it is not immediately threatening. Except in the cases of violent death from accidents, we can make plans about the process of dying; and even in the case of sudden death we can think through what we want to have happen after we die.

There is the financial planning in the face of any kind of death, and there are many people who have done nothing in this regard. It seems obvious that everyone should have a will, simply to make sure that whatever is valuable in our possession will go to those whom we love; intelligent decisions about one's will, especially in regard to children, can avoid excess taxes. Refusal to make a will may be a sign of denial or fear of death, and it certainly may lead to financial harm for our descendants. The same is true of insurance; it is possible to be both overinsured and underinsured, and insurance policies can be selected to provide for the flexibility needed for maximum protection at the time of need without undue cost. Policies to protect a breadwinner from accidental death are also part of planning for death. Furthermore, intelligent planning includes knowing what one's pensions will accomplish for survivors after death. In middle

---

[2] John P. Brantner, *Death Education,* ed. Betty R. Green and Donald P. Irish (Cambridge, Mass.: Schenkman, 1971), pp. 25–26. Used by permission.
[3] See Weisman, *On Dying and Denying,* p. 135.

life, especially, a person may have acquired debts or mortgages which could eliminate the estate; there are ways of insuring the payment of such debts. In some cases, also, steps may be taken to guarantee payments of extended medical expenses and even death and funeral costs. Often such items are merely overlooked in the normal expectation of a long life, but intelligent understanding that death may occur at any time suggests that such steps are part of one's responsibilities.

THE PROCESS OF DYING

The most important element in the process of dying is to be treated as a human being with as much control remaining in one's hands as is possible in light of one's condition. The impersonal and technological aspects of hospital care often get in the way of interpersonal relations, although this is not necessarily so. Especially when a patient is listed as hopeless, there is a tendency on the part of physicians and staff to avoid the dying person. Or perhaps many desperate measures are taken to maintain life even when there is no chance that this will mean a return to meaningful existence.[4] Often when the patient is ready to die such measures unnecessarily prolong his life.

Doctors sometimes have to make difficult choices about continuing certain treatments that will prolong life or discontinuing them so that the patient may die peacefully. Dr. Walter Alvarez has deep convictions about the right of the patient to die. By this he does not mean "mercy killing" but only allowing a person to conclude unbearable suffering and meaningless bodily continuance. Sometimes inadequate painkillers are used to keep the dying person from becoming a drug addict![5]

Those who have no fear of death have a fear of long

---

[4] See Richard G. Dumont and Dennis C. Foss, *The American View of Death: Acceptance or Denial?* (Cambridge, Mass.: Schenkman, 1972), pp. 37–38.
[5] See Walter C. Alvarez, in Carl G. Carlozzi, *Death and Contemporary Man* (Grand Rapids: Eerdmans, 1968), pp. 8–13.

drawn out painful experiences in the process of dying. Those who wish to plan their own dying may sign what is called a "living will," which instructs family, physician, clergyman, and lawyer of one's wishes:

If the time comes when I can no longer take part in decisions for my own future, let this statement stand as the testament of my wishes: If there is no reasonable expectation of my recovery from physical or mental disability, I, ———, request that I be allowed to die and not be kept alive by artificial means or heroic measures. Death is as much a reality as birth, growth, maturity, and old age—it is the one certainty. I do not fear death as much as I fear the indignity of deterioration, dependence and hopeless pain. I ask that drugs be mercifully administered to me for terminal suffering even if they hasten the moment of death.

This request is made after careful consideration. Although this document is not legally binding, you who care for me will, I hope, feel morally bound to follow its mandate. I recognize that it places a heavy burden of responsibility on you, and it is with the intention of sharing that responsibility and of mitigating any feelings of guilt that this statement is made.[6]

Another choice, which may be tied in with a "living will," is to die at home. When one is released from a hospital, it is possible to get agreement from one's family and physician that under no circumstances will one be returned to the hospital for further treatment. One may become so helpless that nursing is needed around the clock, and some special devices may be installed in the home, but to many this is better than a return to the hospital. A patient was told that he had about nine months to live; he asked that he be allowed to spend the last days in his son's home, with whatever nursing he required, and that he be allowed to die there. He knew from the moment of his diagnosis that this was what he desired.

---

[6] Euthanasia Educational Council, 250 W. 57th St., New York, N.Y. 10019. Used by permission.

Another possible choice is just beginning to become available, which is to enter a "hospice," which might be defined as a place for terminal patients who will receive all the medical care they need during the process of dying. (The word hospice is a medieval term for a community that cares for travelers on the way.) One example of this is the Home for Dying Destitutes in Calcutta. Here the problem was not lingering death in a hospital but that of dying on the street. The dying are picked up from the streets and taken to the home, which is a former temple of the goddess Kali, where they can either die or recover in an atmosphere of love. The genius behind this is Mother Teresa, an Albanian from Yugoslavia who with her cohorts includes this ministry to the dying as part of their work with the poor. An outsider entering this home would probably be struck first with horror and repulsion, mixed with a degree of pity; then would come a genuine compassion; and finally, he would see these poor, desolate and dying men and women, some of them lepers with stubs in place of hands, as dear and delightful friends. There is, in Mother Teresa's ministry, an outpouring of Christian love as she sees the Christ in every human being, and this is what one should know when he is in the process of dying, for then he knows himself as a human being with dignity under God. Mother Teresa's religious order is growing, and new work has been started in many Indian villages and towns, in Australia, and in Latin America.[7]

In 1967 Dr. Cicely Saunders opened Saint Christopher's Hospice just outside of London. The purpose was to enable dying persons to maintain their relationships with others, to manage pain creatively, and to provide an atmosphere where dignity of the human person continued to the moment of death. With this philosophy, it is normal for patients to remain at home with their families as long as possible.

When the patient finally goes to the hospice, he is not

[7] See Malcolm Muggeridge, *Something Beautiful for God* (New York: Harper & Row, 1971), for the story of Mother Teresa.

treated impersonally and there are no great heroics in prolonging life. The emphasis is still on the continuance of human relationships, even if this might lead to a slightly shorter life. Instead of reliance being on intravenous feeding, a more able patient might feed one who is weaker, which takes more time but enables the sicker patient to feel wanted and the more able one to do something useful. Pain management is worked out carefully so that one gets sufficient dosage to keep pain from recurring rather than receiving medication only when pain becomes unendurable. The patient therefore can concentrate on relating to other people instead of on the expectation of recurring pain.

This approach to death is religious, for God is seen as working through interpersonal relationships, where people give themselves to each other. The relationships between staff and patients become close, which strengthens both groups. There is a chapel with services for those who wish them.[8]

For those facing long terminal illnesses, a hospice is the answer. It still does not take care of patients who are dying quickly from a disease that needs constant treatment, or those who are losing the battle against death when there is a chance of success. For those who are going to get well and for those who can benefit from all the medical skills available, a hospital is called for. There is a place for the heroics of modern medicine for many of us, and we must never forget to give thanks for what medical science has accomplished.

The hospice serves a different purpose, and the conflict arises when the hospital is asked to do what a hospice can do much better. But there are few hospices in the world.

A hospice is being planned for New Haven, Connecticut. It will operate primarily in homes, with inpatient beds when living at home becomes too difficult for patient and family. The goal is stated as follows:

---

[8] See J. William Worden, "The Right to Die," *Pastoral Psychology*, June 1972, pp. 13–14; Cicely Saunders, "The Moment of Truth: Care of the Dying Person," *Death and Dying*, ed. L. Pearson (Cleveland: Case Western Reserve Press, 1969), pp. 49–78.

The Hospice doors will be open to everyone, regardless of the individual's ability to pay. The patient's course will be determined by his or her own life style, and the patients and families will take an active role in the decision making process and the work. The method of care will depend on the scientific management of symptoms. By relieving the physical, mental, spiritual and/or social distress; by managing pain, nausea, anxiety, depression, fear of the unknown and concern for their families, patients will be helped to garner strength for living and for doing what is important to them as life comes to a close.

The team which collaborates with family and patient will include people from many professional disciplines as well as other caring individuals. We believe patients and their families together with staff and volunteers can do this best in a community which shares the work and provides a system for support and mutual understanding. We recognize that those who help the terminally ill, whether family, friend or worker, expend tremendous energy which needs replenishment. Therefore, the quality of the ongoing worker relations, especially in their openness and concern for one another, is essential to sustain the Hospice community.[9]

This New Haven model may prove a guide for an American approach to death, as have Cicely Saunders' hospice in Great Britain and Mother Teresa's Home for Dying Destitutes in India and elsewhere.

PLANNING YOUR FUNERAL

Part of one's death rehearsal is planning what will happen to your body after death, for there are plenty of alternatives. The dying person often has strong preferences, and these can be made known through written instructions placed with one's will, with a clergyman or lawyer, or with the family. Such prearrangement may be a form of hostility to make the survivors refrain from the kind of funeral they want. Or it may be a mature conclusion about the meaning of life, which may or may not be shared by one's family.

---

[9] Published by Hospice Inc., New Haven, Conn. Used by permission.

Whatever happens at your funeral, you need to remember that a funeral is a rite of passage marking the completion of your life and the social character of your existence. It is the grief-stricken ones whom you love who will benefit or suffer from your funeral—not you. So rather than try to control them on a postmortem basis, your funeral plans should take them and their wishes into consideration. This is best accomplished by free and open discussion in which your position and theirs are brought into dialogue.

The service and the disposal of the body contribute to the overcoming of grief, and the question facing us is which approaches are most effective and meaningful in a rapidly changing society. Does someone have to see the body to be convinced either of the reality of death or to begin "grief work"? Can there be a modern service without the body that will be just as effective? What about nonreligious memorial services? We do not have all the answers, and they vary with different points of view about the meaning of death as well as the handling of the emotions of grief.

The traditional American approach has been a church funeral followed by burial. The historic liturgies are still meaningful to many people in all traditions. Some Catholics believe that a requiem mass is essential, and that burial should be in a church-owned cemetery, with cremation still a doubtful solution. Many Protestants still prefer a traditional service followed by burial. Often bodies are transported to distant points to be buried in a family grave site.

There are others who want a religious service, but prefer to have it in a funeral chapel, sometimes because there is no church connection. This may be followed by either burial or cremation. In some cases, there is only a graveside or crematorium service.

Another possibility is a service worked out either by a dying person or by his family that represents their view of death. Where there is strong aversion to the church's teaching about resurrection or immortality, there may be a desire to focus the service on the meaning of the life just closed, with the insertion of selections from recent literature and Bible passages that do not refer to an afterlife.

Then there are services without a body. This may occur in case of destruction of the body through accident or fire by necessity. In other cases cremation or burial may quite properly precede a service, so that the funeral becomes also a memorial service; then there is usually a brief service at the grave site or crematorium at the time of disposal.

Another option, becoming more popular, is the donation of the body or organs to a medical school. In such cases, whatever remains after the corpse has been investigated or the organs transplanted may be cremated and the ashes returned, or they may be disposed of in any way the family wishes. It is possible in most states to file one's statement about donating one's body with state officials and to carry with one a statement that at death the body is to be transported to a medical school. This, it seems to many, is a sensible way to be of value to mankind after one's death.

Such decisions are not always made on a rational basis. There may be neurotic feelings about the fear of worms or of fire that make any plans for disposing of the body difficult to carry out. This may be one reason for the popularity of metal caskets which are protected by concrete in the grave or by marble slabs in mausoleums. But if the return is that of ashes to ashes and dust to dust, the decomposition of the body by natural means is to be desired.

The best of plans may be upset by accidents or war or travel. If a person has offered his body for medical research and dies in an airplane crash, new plans may have to be improvised. If a person is killed in war in a foreign land, someone has to decide whether to have the body buried or cremated overseas or brought home. Travel often leads to similar difficulties, and the cost of transporting a body from someplace such as Indonesia, plus the red tape, may be prohibitive. In any case, some of us think, why shouldn't a person have his final rest where he died?

The increased elaboration and rising cost of funerals,

sometimes approaching the indecent in terms of good taste, have led to the rise of memorial societies. They are working for simpler funerals and lower costs and are seeking cooperation from funeral directors, who sometimes refuse to respond. The idea is to use a simple wooden casket or box, to eliminate the extravagant use of flowers, to have a simple religious service, and to keep down costs. Because of the entrenched interests of both undertakers and florists, progress has been slow, but as the societies grow in number they have been able to make increasing demands.

There are also secular funeral societies who are seeking to do away with all traditional practices and who favor quick burial, cremation, or donation of the body, with no religious service of any kind. The body is gone, and all one can do is work out one's own grief.

Anyone who has lived for any length of time in India comes to a new appreciation of cremation. In that land, which has the largest population except for China, burial would mean extremely large cemeteries. The Hindu answer is cremation followed by dropping the ashes in the Ganges or some other holy river. One sees a funeral procession with the body marching through the streets to the open crematorium at the edge of the river; the family watches over the burning and places the ashes in the river—and it is a religious ceremony.

We can learn a good deal from a traditional jazz band funeral which is part of the ritual in New Orleans among jazz musicians. After the church service and the procession to the cemetery, the cortege is met by a jazz band which leads the body to the grave site playing a dirge. In the working out of grief, such tunes as "Free as a Bird," "Nearer My God to Thee," and "Lead Me Savior" are likely choices. But once the body is in the grave and the minister has pronounced the committal, the drummer takes his handkerchief out of the snare drum, the cornet player sets the theme, and the band starts marching down South Rampart Street playing "Oh, Didn't He Ramble," "Just a Closer Walk with

Thee," "Lord, Lord, Lord," or "When the Saints Go Marching In." Thus the mourners move from grief to hope in the resurrection. We respond to such music with our emotions, and we feel both the grief and the confidence expressed by the musicians. Perhaps we can match such feelings with hymns such as "The Strife Is O'er, the Battle Done" or the Vaughan Williams tune for "For All the Saints Who from Their Labors Rest," provided the beat is right. It is harder to catch the spirit of the dirge prior to the burial, when the dissonance and rhythm are essential. Perhaps it take a jazz band, reflecting the theology of black churches, to remind us of what a Christian funeral service ought to be.

My wife and I have talked it over in our family with our children. We know what we would prefer. We have a "living will" because we don't want to live past the stage when it is really living; we carry a card saying that in the case of death our bodies should be taken to the Yale Medical School; and we want a service in the church for anyone who wants to come, with hymns suggesting something joyful, with selections from the burial office of *The Book of Common Prayer* (with certain deletions); and I would like to have an old-time Dixieland band there to play "When the Saints Go Marching In." If there is an accident, we would want to be cremated where it happened and our ashes scattered, with a service in our home church. This is our choice, but it may not be yours.

We will say more about religious beliefs and death in chapters 8 and 9. It may be enough here to point to the central religious belief that love stands at the center of reality, even though it is mocked at every turn. The will to love is stronger even than the will to live, so that we can say that life is finite but that love endures. But it is love that makes us vulnerable to both our own death and to the deaths of others. We never know how deep love can be until we experience someone's death. "Abraham Maslow is profoundly right," says Rollo May, "when he wonders whether we could love passionately if we knew we'd never die."[10] Mythological love affairs among the undying gods may seem insipid for that reason. "Love is not only enriched by our sense of mortality but constituted by it," says May.[11]

That is why some kind of funeral or memorial service is so important. Dying means the loss of those whom we love, and we have to work out this grief in the process of dying. Death also means for the survivors the loss of one who is loved, and the funeral is a form of recall as well as of prayer that helps in our "grief work" and commits the one who is loved to a God who is love. If we have any "intimations of immortality" or "glimpses of eternal life" they may come at this time.

---

[10] Rollo May, *Love and Will* (New York: W. W. Norton & Co., 1969), p. 102. Used by permission.
[11] Ibid.

CHAPTER EIGHT

The Church and
the Dying

On the eastern side of a mosque in the ancient Muslim city of Fatepur-Sikra, built by the great Indian emperor Akbar (1542–1605), there is an inscription in Arabic:

> Jesus, on whom be peace, has said:
> "This world is a bridge.
> Pass over it. But build not your dwelling there."[1]

We do not know how the inscription got there or whether it is an authentic saying. The best guess is that because Akbar was interested in all religions, one of the Portuguese Jesuit priests from Bombay quoted it in an audience with Akbar. It is not unlike an early Jewish saying: "This world is like an antechamber to the world to come; prepare yourself in the antechamber, that you may be admitted to the banqueting hall."[2]

The church has always been interested in its ministry to the dying. Often it has interpreted this world as a "vale of tears" and has promised a better life in the world to come. Yet Christianity has never belittled the process of "passing over the bridge," for it has seen life on earth as crucial and

---

[1] Quoted in Joachim Jeremias, *Unknown Sayings of Jesus* (New York: Macmillan, 1957), p. 99.
[2] Quoted in ibid., p. 100; from *Pirke Aboth* 4:16.

95

meaningful, and it has recognized that death is the end of this life. It has taught confidence in a God of love as the answer to all problems, including that of death.

THE MINISTRY TO THE DYING

When one is dying, there are four professions that minister to him. First and foremost, of course, is the physician, whose task is to be a channel to the healing power of God. His skill is in the healing arts and he seeks in every way at his command to assist in our recovery from illness. He therefore sees the death of a patient as a defeat and is tempted to use all kinds of heroics just to keep one's body alive. But he is more than this, for his ministry includes the dying and all their needs. Because the physician has been a trusted friend when death was not in focus, he can make the transition to sympathetic counselor when the patient knows he is at death's door. We can make our last wishes known to him, so that we may experience the process of dying with as little pain as possible, at a suitable time of our own choosing without losing our humanity, and with continued faith in God.

A second profession that ministers to the dying is the nurse. Many nurses have a natural sympathy with those who suffer, and thus they are able to minister to bodily needs at any time, to provide pain-killing drugs, to make us comfortable, and to listen to us or sense our wishes when we can no longer speak. The nurse's concern, like the physician's, reflects expertise in our physical well-being, but it goes beyond the bodily to a concern for the whole person.

A third profession concerned with the dying is the undertaker. But normally he does not come into the picture until death has occurred and then his relations are with the bereaved only. He starts his ministry at the point where the physician's and nurse's ends. But in some cases the dying person has already made contact with the undertaker so that his wishes will be carried out. Except in cases where the patient has made specific plans to donate his body or organs to a medical institution, the undertaker is involved.

A fourth profession has a ministry both to the dying and the bereaved. The clergyman, either as one's pastor or as hospital chaplain, represents the church and the Christian faith in a ministry to the dying. His wide experience, his clinical training as part of his professional education, and his Christian faith provide resources that can help us. He is not going to convert many patients on their deathbeds, and knows enough not to try. But he is equipped to listen to us, to sense our deep religious longings, and to respond to us at the point where we most need help.

The clergyman is a member of the healing team in a supportive role. He can assist the dying person to guard against magical thinking, for in our bargaining mood we often try to make deals with God or the devil, and in such desperate deals we lose sight of the positive meaning of death. If we really want to die as a mature person who is facing reality, the clergyman can assist us in the interpretation of death and in developing an emotional attitude that helps us overcome fear and anxiety.

Usually we need more help with our emotions than with our intellect. There may be deep feelings of guilt or failure, sins committed against others or good deeds we meant to do and somehow did not find time for, that disturb us. Dag Hammarskjöld put it this way:

Tomorrow we shall meet,
Death and I—
And he shall thrust his sword
Into one who is wide awake.

But in the meantime how grievous the memory
Of hours frittered away.[3]

[3] From *Markings,* by Dag Hammarskjöld, p. 6. Copyright © 1964 by Alfred A. Knopf, Inc. and Faber & Faber, Ltd. Reprinted by permission of the publishers.

For some who are at home in the traditional rituals, there are forms of confession and absolution that may be helpful. For others, just the opportunity to talk things through is important, which is why the clergyman needs to be a good listener, for he needs not only to hear what we are saying but also to understand what we mean by our words. Often the offering of reassurance may come too soon and seem automatic. We need the kind of situation in which we can reveal as much of ourselves as we desire, and then to find out that God accepts us as we are, which is often symbolized by the clergyman's acceptance of us as we are.

What, then, does the minister bring to the dying person? In his concern for the patient the minister is illustrating by his action his faith in every person as a child of God. His own religious confidence is demonstrated by the fact that he will listen to the dying person. He does not preach or argue, unless the patient expresses a specific desire for this approach. The minister does not expect agreement, but he ministers in whatever way is acceptable, perhaps by prayer, by being quiet, and sometimes by reassuring the patient. Cabot and Dicks write:

We would go to a person who is dying whether he accepts any of these beliefs or not. We would go whether he was dying or not; and we would not bring undue pressure either on the physician or patient to have him know the seriousness of his condition. We would go for two reasons: first, because of the need one knows to be present in almost any person who is dying —the need to have despair stamped from his mind, to have his loneliness assuaged, and his deepest desires expressed. Secondly, because it is the least the minister can do in the light of the New Testament, in the light of the personality of Christ and his devotion to all sufferers.[4]

Beside the four professions who minister to the dying,

---

[4] Richard C. Cabot and Russell L. Dicks, *The Art of Ministering to the Sick* (New York: Macmillan, 1936), p. 313. Used by permission.

there are family and friends who come to see the patient out of love, concern, duty, or a mixture of motives. They may or may not be helpful. Usually, however, the supportive role of being with somebody, anybody, is helpful in the loneliness and pain of dying.

Christianity places emphasis on life as meaningful, however, and even as it faces death it is not life-denying, as are some other religions. Swami Vivekananda, the great Indian sage, wrote that "we must be free from death; and to be free from death, we must be free from life. Life is but a dream of death. Where there is life, there will be death; so get away from life if you would be free of death."[5] Opposed to this is the Christian emphasis, which sees life in relation to death and death in relation to new life. As Sydney Evans says, "To live the Christian life in the world, is already to live in some degree beyond death in a faith relationship to him who is alive for us beyond his own death."[6] Even death, says Paul, cannot separate us from the love of God (Romans 8:39).

We cannot learn this in a last-minute deathbed scene, except in rare circumstances. But we can learn it in our own way as we learn the art of dying prior to the final crisis. It is for this reason that it is helpful to look carefully at the varieties of views of death in the Bible.

DEATH IN THE BIBLE

Behind the church's teachings about dying, death, and life after death is the great variety of beliefs portrayed in the Bible. These interpretations sometimes conflict with each other, for they are conditioned by the times in which they were written, by the pressure of opposing views that need to be refuted, and by the influence of views from other

---

[5] *Complete Works*, 8:59, cited in *Religion and Society* (Bangalore), XVIII, 2 (July 1971), p. 4.
[6] "Christian Ministry to the Dying," *Expository Times*, Oct. 1966, pp. 8–9, cited in *Religion and Society*, p. 10.

cultures. For example, there is nothing about resurrection in Jewish thought until the beliefs of Zoroastrianism came into the picture from Persia. Teachings about immortality came into the New Testament from Greek thought. Modification of ideas about a resurrection and the end of the world led to the emphasis in the Fourth Gospel on eternal life. Death is seen as both a natural event and as an enemy, as due to God's economy and to sin. We need to think about Sheol, Hades, Gehenna, heaven, and hell.

The earlier portions of the Jewish Bible take a realistic view of death. In Psalm 90, so often read at burial services for the old, we read:

> Our lifetime is cut short by your anger;
>> our life comes to an end like a whisper.
> Seventy years is all we have—
>> eighty years, if we are strong;
> yet all they bring us is worry and trouble;
>> life is soon over, and we are gone.
>
> —Psalm 90:9–10, TEV

Job puts it even more strongly:

> Man, that is born of woman,
> Is of few days and full of trouble.
> Like a blossom he comes forth and is withered,
> And he flees like the shadow and does not endure. . . .
> And he wastes away like a rotten thing,
> Like a garment which the moth has eaten.
>
> —Job 14:1–2a; 13:28, G

Yet man has a choice, for life is real and death stands as a judgment:

I call heaven and earth to witness against you today that I have put life and death before you, the blessing and the curse; therefore choose life, that you as well as your descendants may live, by loving the Lord your God, by heeding his injunctions, and by

holding fast to him; for that will mean life to you, and a long
time to live upon the land which the Lord swore to your fathers,
Abraham, Isaac, and Jacob, to give them.

—Deuteronomy 30:19–20, G

This promise of life, however, is not for life after death.
Death may be averted for a time, so that "a long time [you
will] live upon the land" as a people and not as an individual.

Life is the primary focus for the Hebrew mind. We see it
as a "unit of vital power," a total person who is active at
every level of mind, body, and spirit. As Genesis has it:
"Then the Lord God molded man out of the dust of the
ground, and breathed into his nostrils the breath of life, so
that man became a living being (Gen. 2:7, G)." We are
talking about a physical body which is a self, a spirit, a
breathing organism which is both mind and body. It is not
a body first in which spirit is incarnated, it is not divided
into two or three parts. It is "an animated body."[7]

"Death," says Silberman, "is to be understood as the
dissolution of this unit. Its aliveness has drained away . . .
yet this dissolution is not utter extinction."[8] So the dead end
up in some kind of shadowy existence in Sheol; they are no
longer alive, they are dead, but they exist. It is to this condition that David refers when he faces the death of his son.
"Can I bring him back again? I shall go to him; he will not
come back to me (2 Sam. 12:23, NEB)." As the psalmist
writes:

What man shall live and not see death
or save himself from the power of Sheol?

—Psalm 89:48, NEB

Sheol is a place of despair, which offers nothing to one who

---

[7] See Lou H. Silberman, "Death in the Hebrew Bible and Apocalyptic Literature," *Perspectives on Death*, ed. Liston O. Mills (Nashville: Abington Press,
1969), pp. 15–19.
[8] Ibid., p. 19.

loves life but may be better than the kind of life Job is having, although even Job prefers life:

> Let him leave me alone, that I may brighten up a little,
> Before I go, never to return,
> To a land of darkness and blackness,
> A land of shadow, like gloom,
> Of blackness without order,
> And when it shines, it is like gloom.
>
> —Job 10:20b–22, G

In the shadows of Sheol there is no experience of God.

> For in death there is no remembrance of thee.
> In Sheol who praises thee?
>
> —Psalm 6:5, G

Yet even Sheol seems to be omitted in this passage:

> Even wise men die;
> The fool and the brutish alike perish,
> And leave their wealth to others.
> Their graves are their everlasting home,
> Their dwelling throughout the ages,
> Though lands are named after them.
> But man is an ox without understanding;
> He is like the beasts that perish.
>
> —Psalm 49:10–12, G

Contrasted with this is the idea of corporate personality, which stressed the family, tribe, and nation as continuing entities. The constant stress on Jewish identity through the ages finds its source in this sense of corporateness as the continuation of life in this world.

But this is not the end of the story, for a new influence came from outside the Jewish tradition and fitted into it. For if those who were "asleep" could be brought to life again in a resurrection, a new view of life after death was born. "And many of those who sleep in the land of dust shall awake, some to everlasting life, and others to everlasting reproach and contempt (Dan. 12:2, G)."

A passage similar to the one from Daniel is found in Isaiah and shows the influence of the same Zoroastrian kind of thinking:

> But thy dead will live, their bodies will rise,
> Those who dwell in the dust will awake, and will sing for
> joy;
> For thy dew is a dew of light,
> And the earth will bring the Shades to birth.
> —Isaiah 26:19, G

Oscar Cullmann points to a direct similarity between these two passages from Daniel and Isaiah and one from 1 Thessalonians. Except for the insertion of Jesus' death and resurrection into the argument, the claim is identical with the Zoroastrian-Jewish view:

We do not want you to be under any misapprehension, brothers, about those who are falling asleep. You must not grieve for them, as others do who have no hope. For if we believe that Jesus died and rose again, then by means of Jesus God will bring back with him those who have fallen asleep. For we can assure you, on the Lord's own authority, that those of us who will still be living when the Lord comes will have no advantage over those who have fallen asleep. For the Lord himself, at the summons, when the archangel calls and God's trumpet sounds, will come down from heaven, and first those who died in union with Christ will rise; then those of us who are still living will be caught up with them on clouds into the air to meet the Lord, and so we shall be with the Lord forever.

> —1 Thessalonians 4:13–17, G[9]

Not only did Persian apocalyptic feed into the stream of Jewish thought but Greek ideas of immortality made their

---

[9] See Oscar Cullmann, "Immortality of the Soul or Resurrection of the Dead?" *Immortality and Resurrection,* ed. Krister Stendahl (New York: Macmillan, 1965), pp. 118–19.

contribution as well, and this also was picked up in the New Testament. The clearest passage showing Greek influence is in the Apocryphal book the Wisdom of Solomon:

> For God created man for immortality,
> And made him the image of his own eternity,
> But through the devil's envy death came into the world,
> And those who belong to his party experience it.
> But the souls of the upright are in the hand of God,
> And no torment can reach them.
> In the eyes of foolish people they seemed to die,
> And their decease was thought an affliction,
> And their departure from us their ruin,
> But they are at peace.
> For though in the sight of men they are punished,
> Their hope is full of immortality,
> And after being disciplined a little, they will be shown great kindness.
> For God has tried them,
> And found them worthy of himself.
>
> —Wisdom of Solomon 2:23—3:5, G

THE NEW TESTAMENT

Four major concepts about death and life after death were influential in the ancient world in New Testament times. The latest arrival on the Jewish scene was belief in the immortality of the soul, which had roots in Egyptian thought. Also recent, but much earlier, was the importation of the Persian concept of future resurrection, with the accompanying views of judgment, heaven, and hell. These were wedded with previous Jewish thinking about the Day of Yahweh, when the nations would be judged, and with the idea of resurrection as the reanimation of dead bodies. All these ideas came together because of the intense suffering of the Jewish nation with the accompanying belief that the nation was chosen of God and could not die.[10]

---

[10] See Frederick C. Grant, *Can We Still Believe in Immortality?* (Louisville: The Cloister Press, 1944), pp. 16–20.

Jesus seems to have taken some sort of belief in resurrection for granted, but he was never very explicit about it because his major concern was for the quality of this life. The idea of the end of the world served as a framework for his thinking, for the kingdom of God was at hand, but his major emphasis was on repentance and faith, which had as much to do with this world as the next. Ethical purity, uprightness, a childlike faith in a righteous and loving God, and unassuming humility and gentleness stood at the center of his requirements for a life that served God and man.[11]

In Luke 13:1–5, Jesus makes it clear that the Galileans killed by Pilate and those killed when the tower fell on them at Siloam did not die because they were more guilty than others, "but unless you repent, you will all of you come to the same end (Luke 13:5, NEB)." Death comes in the same way that rain falls on the just and the unjust. Death is impartial.

The controversy with the Sadducees makes Jesus' position clearer. The Sadducees denied belief in resurrection, because they could not find the teaching in the first five books of the Bible, the Pentateuch. The Pharisees, on the other hand, with a wider basis in scripture as an authority, believed in resurrection. So the Sadducees put Jesus on the spot with their question about "whose wife will she be?" Jesus gives a double answer: first, you do not know the scriptures, and "when people rise from the dead, there is no marrying or being married, but they live as angels do in heaven (Mark 12:25, G)." Furthermore, since God is the God of Abraham, Isaac, and Jacob, he is the God of the living and not of dead men. Obviously, the resurrected life will not be like this one, but unless we know about angels we cannot tell what it will be like. As the patriarchs are also alive and have a living God, clearly Jesus can justify belief in resurrection from Old Testament texts.

Silberman's conclusion is that Jesus stands within the tra-

---

11 Ibid., p. 23; Silberman, "Death in the Hebrew Bible," pp. 36–37.

dition of an apocalyptic view which assumes resurrection and judgment, but does not concentrate on them. He does not consider death a threat to faith in God, but it is obviously real. He does not speculate about death or postresurrection experience. Yet Jesus faced death with agony, although he overcame this fear with confidence in God at the end.[12]

Jesus' death and resurrection placed the idea of the end of the age and the coming of the kingdom of God in a dual interpretation. With Jesus the kingdom had come and yet because Jesus would return the end was not yet. In this framework the emphasis was on a transformed life on this earth, in which God's purposes would be realized. But this expected event of a second coming was delayed, so that questions came up about those who died in the interim or had died previously.

The proclamation of the gospel went first to the Jews, especially in Jerusalem, but there was also an appeal being made to people in the Greek tradition with their heritage of belief in immortality. To both groups the center of the preaching was Jesus' resurrection. Those who are alive participated in the resurrection through their baptism and a new ethical way of life. Furthermore, because of Jesus' resurrection there is the promise of a general resurrection. This becomes the central argument of 1 Corinthians 15, in which Paul seeks to refute the arguments of the Greeks and the Gnostics, who claim that there is an immortality of a bodiless soul, whereas Paul insists that a "new body" is essential to any understanding of an afterlife. Paul never describes what he means by a "spiritual body," but this is understood against the statement that "flesh and blood cannot inherit the kingdom of God, nor does the perishable inherit the imperishable (1 Cor. 15:50, RSV)." Oscar Cullmann says that this means that "deliverance consists not in a release of soul from body but in a release of both from flesh. We are not released from the body; rather the body itself is set

---

[12] Silberman, "Death in the Hebrew Bible," pp. 42–43; see Henry J. Cadbury, *Immortality and Resurrection*, ed. Stendahl, pp. 125–49; Mathew P. John, "Death and Resurrection," *Religion and Society*, June 1971, pp. 12–19.

free."[13] Paul says that "the trumpet will sound, and the dead will be raised imperishable, and we shall be changed. For this perishable nature must put on the imperishable, and this mortal nature must put on immortality (1 Cor. 15:52b–53, rsv)."

Here Paul uses the language of the Greeks and Gnostics, but he is still talking about resurrection. Because it is obvious that the physical body is destroyed, God acts to add something: "this mortal nature must put on immortality." But this is something that will happen in the future, and what happens now is that in this life we overcome "the sting of death," which "is sin," and at the time of the resurrection of all mankind we will "be raised imperishable."

Cullmann insists that "the transformation of the body does not occur immediately after each individual death."[14] The Jewishness of Paul is maintained, and the dead sleep until the resurrection. "*We* wait, and *the dead* wait."[15] Because the latter are asleep, the interim time may be shorter for them than for us, but they are still in time.

Other scholars think that the Greek influence is stronger than this. Leander Keck points out that Paul shifts to the language of immortality; however, he still does not admit of an immortal soul from the beginning but sees it as a gift from God.[16] George Hedley suggests that as soon as one gets away from the resurrection of a *physical* body, one has moved from the Jewish tradition, and that Paul's shift to the language of immortality is actually a substitution of Greek for Jewish thought, although he subtly mixes resurrection and immortality categories.[17]

Whether or not Paul had moved in this direction, certainly the Fourth Gospel did. Here was a whole new direction in interpretation, later than Paul and the other Gospels

---

[13] Oscar Cullman, *Immortality and Resurrection,* ed. Stendahl, p. 27. Used by permission.
[14] Ibid., p. 37.
[15] Ibid., p. 45.
[16] See Leander Keck, *Perspectives on Death,* ed. Mills, pp. 77–78.
[17] See George Hedley, *The Symbol of the Faith* (New York: Macmillan, 1948), pp. 141–42.

and dealing with new ways of thinking. Instead of an emphasis on a second coming of Jesus, there is a stress on the coming of the Spirit. There is little discussion of death, but rather a strong emphasis from the beginning on eternal life, based on belief in Jesus and his teachings: "Whoever believes in him may have eternal life (John 3:15, RSV)."[18] This is a belief that leads to ethical action and avoids condemnation.

Eternal life is not interpreted in terms of endless time but as a quality of life here and now. It is a matter of being born again, of being in love with God and one's neighbors, on the basis of having received Jesus' word, for "I am the resurrection and the life; he who believes in me, though he die, yet shall he live, and whoever lives and believes in me shall never die (John 11:25–26a, RSV)."

With the loss of belief in apocalyptic, due to the fact that the end of the world has not yet come, the views of Paul have dropped into disfavor, except as 1 Corinthians 15 is used for its emphasis on immortality. However, the major stress of the Fourth Gospel on eternal life as a quality of this life has not been enough for those who yearn for life after death. The Greek view of the immortality of the soul seems to have become the standard belief through the ages and is reflected in most funeral rituals. But even this view is in doubt today, so that we need to reevaluate the various kinds of hope offered to us as we face death.

THE CHURCH'S TEACHING

The church has been influenced by many forms of thought since the time of the New Testament. We can summarize some of the emphases as follows:

1. Christianity takes this life seriously, not as a bridge but as the locale of meaningful living. Death provides a limit to life and therefore must be faced realistically.

---

[18] See John 3:16–18. See Keck, *Perspectives on Death,* ed. Mills, pp. 80–85.

2. Human life does not automatically transcend death, but through the resurrection of Jesus Christ there is the promise and hope of the gift of new life from a loving God.

3. We do not know much about any life after death, but we have received many images of what it might be like: "the departed live and are conscious and can pray for themselves and others"[19]; there is judgment which may involve an intermediate state; there will be a second coming of Christ, in which all dead and living will be brought together in a final resurrection.[20]

The traditional committal prayer indicates this:

Unto Almighty God we commend the soul of our *brother* departed, and we commit *his* body to the ground; earth to earth, ashes to ashes, dust to dust; in sure and certain hope of the Resurrection unto eternal life, through our Lord Jesus Christ; at whose coming in glorious majesty to judge the world, the earth and the sea shall give up their dead; and the corruptible bodies of those who sleep in him shall be changed, and made like unto his own glorious body; according to the mighty working whereby he is able to subdue all things unto himself.[21]

Even the most orthodox believers have trouble with this prayer, with its mixture of most of the teachings in the New Testament. Many clergy simply do not use it. But it stands as a witness to where the church has been in its teachings.

Yet religious faith is essential for most of us for understanding death and for assistance, both emotional and intellectual, in facing the termination of life. After a careful study of dying patients, Cabot and Dicks come to this conclusion: "Religion may transcend death; some religion does. . . . The tragedy or the victory of death is in the way one dies, not the fact of death itself."[22] What hope do we have?

---

[19] See Grant, *Can We Still Believe in Immortality?* p. 58.
[20] See John, "Death and Resurrection," pp. 18–19.
[21] *Book of Common Prayer*, p. 333.
[22] Cabot and Dicks, *The Art of Ministering to the Sick*, pp. 302, 314.

CHAPTER NINE

Hope

H ope has to do with the future, with expectations about which there is no evidence but about which there is desire. Human beings derive meanings from their past and present and project them into their future, including their survival after death. Hope may operate in terms of the near future, concerning tomorrow's picnic without rain or a promotion at the end of the year or the birth of a baby in nine months. Hope also operates in terms of the remote future, in terms of a college freshman looking forward to his job and marriage, in terms of young parents and their expectations in twenty-five years when they will become grandparents, or of the condition of the nation after their deaths. Hope is related to anticipation and fulfillment. Believers in God expect that God's activity makes for well-being in their lives and for progress in history. "But there is no guarantee of progress in the short run, and in the long run it is inevitable that life on this planet will become extinct."[1] Yet believers claim that God has a future, and they hope that they may in some way share in that future after death.

---

[1] John B. Cobb, Jr., "What Is the Future? A Process Perspective," *Hope and the Future of Man*, ed. Ewert H. Cousins (Philadelphia: Fortress Press, 1972), p. 7. Used by permission.

Even if we have a world view that includes the possibility of life after death, we have no empirical evidence to back up such a conclusion; it contradicts our current view of the psychosomatic unity of man; it seems to stress an inflation of the individual ego; and ethically its otherworldliness weakens our moral perceptions about individual and social responsibility. There is evidence, however, that regardless of what one believes happens after death, there can be hope placed in the proximate future among those who know that they are dying, as the evidence of Elisabeth Kübler-Ross makes clear. Sometimes this is an unrealistic hope for recovery in spite of the evidence, and sometimes it is a more realistic hope that one will be enabled by his or her belief in God or trust in the doctor (or both) to go through the process of dying while maintaining one's dignity, humanity, and faith.[2]

STATUS OF BELIEF IN THE AFTERLIFE

Belief in God does not necessarily lead to belief in an afterlife, and in rare cases there may be belief in life after death without belief in God. In 1968 many studies were made in Europe, and among the population in general (including some religious people associated with religious institutions) a majority believed in God and only a minority in an afterlife. Some sample results are as follows:

In France, 73 percent believed in God and only 35 percent believed in life after death. It was higher in some countries, with Greece having 96 percent who believed in God and 57 percent in an afterlife. Between 1947 and 1968 there were considerable changes in the proportions. In Great Britain in 1947, 49 percent believed in the afterlife, and by 1968 only 38. In the Netherlands, when broken down by religious affiliation, results were highest in the Reformed Church, 97 percent, 72 percent for Catholics, and 76 percent for others. The variations in age-groups in Germany ran

[2] See Elisabeth Kübler-Ross, *On Death and Dying* (New York: Macmillan, 1969), pp. 138–42.

from a low of 45 percent for age 25–34 to 56 percent for age 60–70. In a sample in the United States, believers ran from 26 percent among Congregationalists to 65 percent among Southern Baptists. That there is confusion as to what is believed is indicated by the following: persons believing that God exists came to 86 percent; that Jesus rose, 67 percent; that death is entry to eternal life, 65 percent; that after death you will live forever, 55 percent; that you will rise again, 44 percent. Among those who would ask for a religious burial, only 31 percent said they are *certain* of an afterlife, and 14 percent said they do not believe in an afterlife, and 22 percent that they do not believe in their resurrection; so they will keep the tradition even if they don't believe.[3]

There is a greater crisis than we might have predicted in the area of religious hope for an afterlife. Ninian Smart suggests three major roots. First, the scientific study of the scriptures has eroded many methods of argument based on scriptural authority, and has replaced them with a historical orientation that strengthens faith as such but demands a new kind of doctrinal thinking. Second, the rise of scientific thinking has provided a world view that differs widely from biblical views, and therefore it is impossible to use geographical language in relation to heaven and hell or other concepts. Third, new views of man based on anthropology, sociology, and psychology have eliminated the body-soul dualism that supported beliefs in immortality and have made resurrection of the body highly unlikely. All this has also led to mythological interpretations of much of the imagery of life after death, thus supporting the whole process of scepticism toward an afterlife.[4]

This approach has led some theologians to a positive acceptance of death because they see it as a means to the triumph of creativity as the work of God in the world. Perhaps

---

[3] See the charts and tables, which give far more information, in André Godin, ed., *Death and Presence* (Brussels: Lumen Vitae Press, 1972), pp. 17–38.
[4] See Ninian Smart, "Death and the Decline of Religion in Western Society," Arnold Toynbee et al., *Man's Concern with Death* (London: Hodder and Stoughton, 1968), pp. 139–40.

the strongest form of this argument comes from Henry Nelson Wieman, who writes that "except for death, creativity would have died long ago." He argues that

> without death, new generations could not arise ... the human race could not recover and deepen that learning in depth which is the genius of the newly born.... Humanity would lose that tender concern which is awakened in the adult by love and care for infants and little children.... Youth could not arise to break through the hardening crust of class stratification, institutional fixation, and rigid habit formation.... Vivid awareness of the unique individual swiftly flowering and soon to fade would not be with us.... We could never attain that comprehensive perspective of the individual's whole life which can be had only after the irrelevancies, trivialities, and inconsistencies of bodily existence have ended.... The creativity of life would sink and disappear beneath the dull routine of conformity.... The accumulation of created good in the life of the individual would submerge and smother his concern for creativity.... This makes it possible [for a person] to offer up his life in its wholeness, including his death, to the creativity which unites God and man.[5]

Life and death conceived in this way are not without hope. The commitment is to the work of God in this world, and God's work is to sponsor the growth of meaning and value through creative interchange. One's life is given up to God so that God's work may go on unimpeded by those who through old age and infirmity would finally be in the way. Life, because it operates within undefined and unpredictable limits, has value and meaning that contribute to ultimate meaning.

PSYCHOLOGICAL STUDIES

Hope is a quality of mind or an attitude that implies that we can change the world a little bit. It means that when we

[5] Henry Nelson Wieman, *The Empirical Theology of Henry Nelson Wieman*, ed. Robert W. Bretall (New York: Macmillan, 1963; Southern Illinois Press paperback), pp. 106–8. Used by permission.

are face to face with death we can maintain our healthy and meaningful relationships with the doctors and nurses, the clergy, and our family and friends. In some cases, it involves a chance for survival of at least this illness, or a temporary regression. Hope may be related to the desirability of either survival or death. It is at this level that we have psychological studies of the nature of hope, of the means whereby we can assist in keeping hope alive, and of the relation of hope to the fact of death. Religiously, the approach to death as a means to the furtherance of God's work in the world, as in Wieman's interpretation, is psychologically understandable.

But is this limitation necessary? If one accepts it dogmatically, as many psychologists do, then any "investigation of what happens after death becomes a silly thing to do."[6] Even if, as statistics show, many church people no longer believe in life after death, there must be strong reasons why traditional theology has always included some kind of belief in resurrection or immortality, why funeral services commit the soul to God and the body to the ground, and speak of the reunion of loved ones in heaven. Such reasons may be studied psychologically. They may be the projection of desires for continued life; they may arise in the unconscious, for the unconscious always assumes its own immortality; or they may be intimations of immortality that result from the values man places on the permanence of his relationship with God and his fellows. We will discover evidence for such psychological interpretations as we look at the arguments for various kinds of life after death.

But there is still a desire for some empirical evidence, something based on experience, something like the experience of the disciples or Paul of the risen Christ, and this turns some psychologists to psychical research. There are numerous cases of awareness of the presence of a person after he has died. Often it is an appearance of someone who speaks to the surviving friend and who wears the exact clothes he had on at the moment of death; yet the friend has

6 Gardner Murphy, *The Meaning of Death*, ed. Herman Feifel (New York: McGraw-Hill, 1959), p. 337.

no way of knowing what peculiar dress was involved, for perhaps the death occurred thousands of miles away.[7] The recounting of a number of such experiences is very impressive, although it is difficult to know what they mean as far as life after death is concerned.[8]

There are reports from those who have been clinically dead and restored to life. There is a sense of being removed from the body, followed by sensations of light, of floating, of bliss and joy, accompanied by ringing of bells. When they are brought back to life, it is something of a shock. Assuredly, the fear of death is removed. Such reports have occurred frequently enough to make us take them seriously.

This is not very different from reports of experiences with drugs. William James once reported on an experience with laughing gas:

With me, as with every other person of whom I have heard, the keynote of the experience is the tremendously exciting sense of an intense metaphysical illumination. Truth lies open to the view in depth beneath depth of almost blinding evidence. The mind sees all the logical relations of being with an apparent subtlety and instantaneity to which its normal consciousness offers no parallel; only as sobriety returns, the feeling of insight fades, and one is left staring vacantly at a few disjointed words and phrases, as one stares at a cadaverous-looking snow-peak from which the sunset glow has just fled, or at the black cinder left by an extinguished brand.[9]

Yet there is a difference, and James describes what genuine mystical awareness is about. It also operates in the subliminal consciousness and is accompanied by visions or lights and lacks content, but it is a rising up of the immanent

---

[7] See Murphy, *The Meaning of Death,* ed. Feifel, p. 338.
[8] See Rosalind Heywood, in Toynbee et al., *Man's Concern with Death,* pp. 185–250, for a report on a variety of psychic experiences and their meaning for belief in life after death.
[9] William James, *The Will to Believe* (New York: Longmans Green & Co., 1896), p. 284n.

God in our midst. For many people, says James, religion *"means* immortality," but there are not enough facts, so that, says James, "I consequently leave the matter open."[10]

Gardner Murphy, likewise a sympathetic interpreter of psychic experience, says,

I do not actually anticipate finding myself in existence after physical death. If this is the answer the reader wants, he can have it. But if this means that in a serious philosophical argument I would plead the antisurvival case, the conclusion is erroneous. I linger because I cannot cross the stream. We need far more evidence; we need new perspectives; perhaps we need more courageous minds.[11]

Both James and Murphy believe that on the basis of psychological evidence there is no firm conclusion on either side of the argument for life after death. Simply because no one has been able to transmit to the living what it means to survive after death, there is no basis for judgment on this level. However, in the past religion has not relied on psychological evidence but on theological corollaries from assertions about the nature of God and the nature of man, usually involving some view of the nature of the soul leading to the possibility of some kind of immortality or resurrection or eternal life or being of value in the memory of God. To these views we now turn.

THE SOUL

The soul, as something different from mind or brain, is difficult to describe or identify. If it is identical with the brain or consciousness, it obviously perishes. If there is a tran-

---

[10] William James, *The Varieties of Religious Experience* (New York: Longmans Green & Co., 1902), p. 524.

[11] Gardner Murphy, *Challenge of Psychical Research* (New York: Harper & Row, 1961), p. 273, quoted by Rosalind Heywood, in Toynbee et al., *Man's Concern with Death*, p. 245. Used by permission.

scending consciousness other than the brain, it may be capable of surviving physical death.

For some people, the soul is identified as that which marks man off from other animals, for the higher animals especially have certain powers of the brain to deal with problems, but the principles of abstract intelligence, freedom, love, and worship are missing, and these are the functions of the soul. It is through these principles that a human being gains his sense of identity. These functions, it is claimed, do not necessarily depend on the body for their continuance, and therefore it is possible to think of them as surviving bodily death. Such a concept of the soul cannot be demonstrated as a scientific fact; it arises rather from the intuition of the meaning of one's life and is often a presupposition arising from the unconscious which serves as the basis for meaningful living.

Lovers talk naturally of the soul or of soul-to-soul communication which operates on a deeper level than scientific communication. Blacks talk of soul, applying the word to soul food or soul language, as something which expresses a racial or cultural unconscious. But in these cases the soul is conceived as embodied, and we still have the problem of imagining what a disembodied soul would be, and how one would identify it. This accounts for the return of many theologians to an emphasis on the resurrection of the body, which, if conceivable, would at least be identifiable.

Soul, suggests Lloyd Geering, is an abstraction which helps to describe a high level of human experience. It points to deep and profound meanings, but its reality still depends on the continuous functioning of the human organism. If the spiritual aspect of man, which is another way of thinking of soul, depends on the physical organism for our identification, there is no way for one to conceive that it will survive the cessation of life of the organism.[12]

---

[12] See Lloyd Geering, *God in the New World* (Valley Forge: Judson Press, 1968), p. 53.

IMMORTALITY

Throughout the history of Christianity, belief in either immortality or resurrection was pretty much taken for granted. Because of the influence of Greek thought on theology, there was a dominance of belief in some kind of immortality, so that the soul of a believer went straight to heaven (often conceived symbolically rather than literally as simply being in the presence of God). Without any effort, it was possible to think of soul or spirit as having a continuing identity, and receiving judgment from God in the light of faith and behavior on earth. At times this belief was complicated by concepts of heaven, hell, and limbo; and sometimes the New Testament view of a last judgment was combined with an immediate but provisional judgment at death. The idea of the dead sleeping until the Day of the Lord dropped out of sight. Purgatory was attacked at the time of the Reformation, so that Protestants were left with a single judgment at death, with high requirements for making heaven.

For the modern man, arguments for immortality do not rest so much on the nature of the soul as on the nature of God. If the creativity of God is seen in the event of birth, and birth is seen as the emergence into a new life which is beyond the imagination of the fetus or newborn infant, then we can see this same creativity of God at work in death, which is birth into a new life that is equally beyond the imagination of someone living on earth.

Another argument, associated with Teilhard de Chardin, begins with a view of man as evolving toward becoming fully human and toward becoming a personalized spirit which will never die. Any study of the emergence of the universe points to an open-ended continuing of the process in a way that is beyond man's imagining, and yet the evidence of such development is overwhelming. The body, which is limited by space and time, is freed from such limitations, so that we do not need to struggle with such problems. A "spiritual body" is freed from flesh and blood, from space and time, and exists in the presence of God, who also is freed from such limits. Lepp says:

Not everyone will enjoy eternal life to the same degree. Those who live in this life at a slower pace and make but modest use of their facilities of knowing and loving will have a proportionate share in eternal life. On the other hand, the *passionate,* those who love and seek truth with enthusiasm and perseverance will continue to grow throughout eternity.[13]

Another kind of argument deriving from the nature of God as unselfish love was given by Douglas C. Macintosh. Such a God

can be depended upon to continue, in spite of physical death, the work he has begun, namely, of moral salvation, of bringing many sons to perfection. He has imposed upon the individual as a duty the moral law of absolute perfection, and this, which is essentially an endless task, makes imperative the demand for unending opportunity.[14]

It is possible that the really degenerate will be given only a conditional immortality. For those who die young, God's love will make up for it in the world to come.[15]

I once summed up the argument this way:

If human personality has ultimate value and if God is the conserver of values, then it is reasonable to suppose that God will provide for the continuance of the human soul or personality in some form or other. We cannot prove this, and we cannot indicate how this is possible, but neither can it be shown to be impossible. It is a corollary to the Christian belief about God

---

[13] Ignace Lepp, *Death and Its Mysteries* (New York: Macmillan, 1968), p. 186; see pp. 154–91.

[14] Douglas Clyde Macintosh, *Theology as an Empirical Science* (New York: Macmillan, 1919), p. 206.

[15] Douglas Clyde Macintosh, *The Reasonableness of Christianity* (New York: Charles Scribner's Sons, 1925), p. 102.

and man. It accounts for some of the undeserved evils in the world, for infant death, for unrealized possibilities in the development of personality, and for the conservation of human values.[16]

Such arguments may be helpful to those already predisposed to believe in immortality, but they have no validity if the presuppositions are not granted. It is possible to believe just as fully in the goodness and love of God and come to the conclusion, as Wieman does, that death serves God's purposes and that human life is fulfilled in serving God rather than in survival after death.

Some who refuse to believe in the immortality of the soul argue for "social" immortality, or the immortality of influence. We see the values in our children, in our achievements, in our relationships, and even in the material assets which we leave behind. We speak glowingly of the inheritance of Gandhi, Martin Luther King, Abraham Lincoln, Florence Nightingale, or Winston Churchill. We take our lead from

> Let us now praise distinguished men,
> Our forefathers before us.
> They are a great glory to the Lord who created them;
> They have shown his majesty from of old. . . .
> There are some of them who have left a name,
> So that men declare their praise;
> And there are some who have no memorial,
> And have perished as though they had not lived,
> And have become as though they had not been,
> With their children after them.
> Yet these were merciful men,
> And their uprightness has not been forgotten.
> With their descendants it will remain,
> A good inheritance for their posterity.
> —Wisdom of Sirach 44:1–2, 8–11, G

---

[16] R. C. Miller, *What We Can Believe* (New York: Charles Scribner's Sons, 1941), p. 140.

This view does not depend on power and prestige, but on love and humility. A mother who brings up her children, a soldier who serves and dies, a worker who has integrity, even a moron who responds as best he can to the world is included in such a list. The problem becomes acute when one knows that what he leaves behind is not worthy of any praise, for his inheritance is not good; but this is also a problem of judgment by God in any other theory of survival.[17]

But this is not really immortality, for we know that any inheritance or influence will die out and sooner or later there will be no record of our having lived. Any so-called immortality that is limited to this earth must cope with the fact that life on this earth will end. We may take satisfaction in our posterity, but it is not endless.

RESURRECTION

Arguments for resurrection usually begin with the Easter story. However they interpret Jesus' resurrection, most Christians accept it and celebrate it in worship at Easter. Some claim that it was a physical, bodily resurrection of the flesh; others interpret the story as an apparition, a spiritual body in Paul's interpretation, or as a psychical experience of the disciples. No matter how it is interpreted, Christians believe that Jesus conquered death or was released from its finality by an act of God. Furthermore, the experience of the disciples meant that they could confidently expect the coming of the kingdom of God in the near future. Through the power of Jesus' resurrection, of Jesus who was the son of God and the Messiah, the disciples believed that they, too, would live; and this belief has been carried over into some current Christian thinking.[18]

Usually the arguments are mixed with those about immor-

---

[17] See Raymond B. Cattell, *Psychology and the Religious Quest* (New York: Thomas Nelson & Sons, 1938), pp. 72–76, cited in Peter Hamilton, *The Living God and the Modern World* (London: Hodder and Stoughton, 1967), p. 130.
[18] See Frederick C. Grant, *Can We Still Believe in Immortality?* (Louisville: The Cloister Press, 1944), pp. 30–34, 128–49.

tality and eternal life, but we have seen that there is a difference. Immortality assumes that there is a soul which can exist separately from the body; eternal life stresses the quality of life as having a timeless and spaceless implication or as simply an aspect of this life in what is called "the eternal now." Resurrection does not utilize these categories, but stresses some kind of restoration to a life of spiritual identity of a person who is totally dead. Usually shorn of any expectation of a general resurrection after an indeterminate period of sleeping, current views of resurrection assume that after death there is a gift of new life, perhaps mixed with judgment. About such a life the New Testament is vague:

> What no eye has seen, nor ear heard,
> nor the heart of man conceived,
> what God has prepared for those who love him.[19]
>
> —1 Corinthians 2:9, RSV

It is suggested that all language about resurrection is symbolic, and to reduce it to nonsymbolic or literal terms is to destroy its meaning. The symbol of the resurrection of the body has value because it points to the significance of both the individual and the social connotations of the meaning of life. Both the individual and the social aspects of life are confronted with God and stand under judgment; yet both also stand under God's grace as they work in and through his creative transforming of the world.[20] According to this view, we can talk of being reborn, of death to the old man and new birth, of dying to sin and rising to new life, and of being transformed as ways of describing what happens in this life.

Today fewer people than in former times believe that bodies are risen from the ground or sea or ashes. Yet the idea of a symbolic rising from the dead, even in terms of Paul's "spiritual body," provides for some believers an ade-

---

[19] See Isaiah 64:4.
[20] See Reinhold Niebuhr, *The Nature and Destiny of Man* (New York: Charles Scribner's Sons, 1943), 1: 308–13.

quate way of thinking about life after death, which is why 1 Corinthians 15 is still meaningful when read at funerals.

ETERNAL LIFE

One meaning of eternal is "outside of or beyond time." Other meanings are similar to infinite or endless time, without beginning or end. Eternity may be thought of as a single "now" at a point of completion. In some cases, the Fourth Gospel ties in the concept of eternal life with the end of the age and some kind of act of God at that point, but normally eternal life is a gift now for some people.

"He who believes in the Son has eternal life; he who does not obey the Son shall not see life, but the wrath of God rests upon him (John 3:36, RSV)." "For this is the will of my Father, that every one who sees the Son and believes in him should have eternal life; and I will raise him up at the last day (John 6:40, RSV)." "He who eats my flesh and drinks my blood has eternal life, and I will raise him up at the last day (John 6:54, RSV)." "And this is the testimony, that God gave us eternal life, and this life is in his son (1 John 5:11, RSV)."

The requirement is to believe that Jesus is the Son of God, so that we are operating entirely within the Christian tradition. There is no reference here to the fate of Abraham, Isaac, and Jacob, of believers in the Jewish or other traditions. Those who so believe have eternal life now, and this is sufficient.

Paul Tillich writes that any view of life after death as "endless future is without a final aim; it repeats itself and could well be described as an image of hell." Time does run toward an end, and if we talk about life after death in images of time we are in trouble. "There is no time *after* time, but there is eternity *above* time."[21] When the Fourth Gospel deals with this problem, it sees Christ as one who comes

[21] Paul Tillich, *The Eternal Now* (New York: Charles Scribner's Sons, 1963), p. 125.

from eternity and returns to eternity. There is a whole new dimension to this kind of thinking, so that Jesus can say, "Before Abraham was, I am (John 8:58, RSV)," which is not a historical statement but a metaphysical one.

A professor of philosophy thinks of it in this way:

Eternal life is primarily a category of the present. And to think of it solely as "afterwards" or "beyond" would certainly be a myth. We gain some experience of eternity every time we have an "enlightening" experience—an experience whereby everything holds together in our existence, some aspect of life finds its purpose, and a relationship with others becomes established and meaningful. . . . Eternal life is not survival but life itself.[22]

This conception of eternity may be a way by which we come to know ourselves as children of God, as mortal and yet as participants in an eternal now that is beyond time. It is a quality of life that has important repercussions for our temporal life. If one has this quality, one becomes contagious, so that one affects others. One who senses the eternal now as a quality recognizes it in others, so that one can never cease to care for those who are less fortunate. One begins to see the value of every human being, because every human being is loved by God.

We love, because he first loved us. If any one says, "I love God," and hates his brother, he is a liar; for he who does not love his brother whom he has seen, cannot love God whom he has not seen. And this commandment we have from him, that he who loves God should love his brother also.

—1 John 4:19–21, RSV

Many people are content to stop at this point, for it fits in with the sense of the holiness of an eternal God, it lets us bury our dead, and it gives meaning to life here and now. But unless we go further, others would claim, and do

---

[22] Godin, ed., *Death and Presence*, pp. 56–57. Used by permission.

as the author of the Fourth Gospel does, which is to accept the promise that those who know eternal life will be raised, they are not satisfied. Then we are back to the point in our thinking at which we have to face the criticisms of belief in resurrection or immortality of the soul.

What we have tried to do so far is to present as fairly as possible the claims made by religious people, particularly in the Christian tradition, about life after death. We have not looked at non-Christian traditions, which also have rich teachings related to the meaning of life and death. We have, to some extent, considered the conclusions of secular-minded scientists who have examined the art of dying and what happens afterwards. There is one more interpretation of death and life after death that needs to be considered, to which we now turn.

GOD'S MEMORY

There is a growing acceptance among theologians of a position known as process theology, in which everything that happens is a process of becoming and perishing in a world in which God is active as loving, forgiving, and growing. God takes upon himself our values, both good and bad; the good he assimilates and the bad he transforms in his own reality. He can be frustrated by the evil that men do, because he grants to mankind a genuine freedom.

In this approach, there is in man a pluralistic aspect: man consists of all the varieties of experience that make up his life history, which is his soul. The soul is the dominant activity in the complex organism which makes up our animal nature; it provides the centralized control. It is like the airport tower that takes in many impulses and sends out many messages, all for the purpose of controlling the activities of the landing and taking off of the planes. Just as there are all kinds of unexpected signals in the tower, so there is novelty in the brain of the human organism. So we can say that "a living person is a soul."

What marks this human soul as different from animals is only a matter of degree, but the differences lead to specific functions. The human soul controls man's capacity for the use of language, for the making of ethical or moral decisions, and for the response of worship in the presence of the holy God. In responding to the lure of God, who attracts men to him, man develops the sense of reverence and duty.

With this functional view of the soul, the question occurs as to whether it can exist apart from the body. Insofar as the soul is a psychophysical organism, it cannot survive the organism's death, and if it could survive we would have to think through what this would mean in terms of space and time, just as we have to do so with the concept of eternal life beyond this life. Furthermore, how would identity of self be maintained in a soul separated from its physical body? And as a final question, if much of what constitutes our lives is in the unconscious or subconscious, how does this fit into the view of soul as a controlling center?[23]

Alfred North Whitehead provides a hint at this point:

The everlasting nature of God, which in a sense is nontemporal and in another sense is temporal, may establish with the soul a peculiarly intense relationship of mutual immanence. Thus in some important sense the existence of the soul may be freed from its complete dependence on the bodily organization.[24]

This may open up the *possibility* of the continuing life of the soul, but it provides no evidence.

There is a sense in which society maintains the identity of those who are dead. George Washington had no existence until he was born, but there is a sense in which he continues as part of our lives; so it is with Lincoln or Lee. Charles Hartshorne sets up his argument in this way:

According to the view I adopt, there was once no such individual as myself, even as something that was "going to exist." But centuries after my death, there will have been that very indi-

---

[23] See John B. Cobb, Jr., *A Christian Natural Theology* (Philadelphia: Westminster Press, 1965), pp. 47–50, 64–91.
[24] Alfred North Whitehead, *Adventures in Ideas* (New York: Macmillan, 1933), p. 267. Used by permission.

vidual which I am. This is creation, with no corresponding de-creation. But, again, what then is death?

Death is the last page of the last chapter of the book of one's life, as birth is the first page of the first chapter. Without a first page there is no book. But given the first page there is, so far, a book. The question of death then is, How rich and how complete is the book to be? It is not a question of reality. The book is already real as soon as the possibility of my death arises; and, as we have argued, reality, whether or not it is created, is indestructible. But truncated books, without suitable extent and proper conclusions, are always possible, until life has continued long enough for the individual's basic purposes to be carried out. Such truncation can be tragic. But it is not even tragic if the entire book is to be annihilated; for then there will have been nothing, not even something tragically broken off and brief. The evil of death presupposes indestructibility of the individual as such. Washington having died is at least Washington. Not just a certain corpse, for by "Washington" we mean a unique unity of experience and decision and thought, and that is no corpse. So those are right who say to themselves upon the death of the loved one: It cannot be that that beloved human reality is now nothing or is now something not human at all.[25]

This sets the stage at some length for Hartshorne's argument. If this book is indestructible, for it to have meaning there needs to be a reader. There are the continuing human beings in future generations who can read it, but this is only the "social" immortality that lasts awhile and then vanishes. Furthermore, human readers cannot grasp the whole book.

"In short," concludes Hartshorne, "our adequate immortality can only be God's omniscience of us. He to whom all hearts are open remains evermore open to any heart that has ever been apparent to him."[26] God reads our lives as they are, omitting nothing and adding nothing, knowing us better

---

[25] Charles Hartshorne, *The Logic of Perfection and Other Essays in Neoclassical Metaphysics* (LaSalle, Ill.: Open Court Publishing Co., 1962), pp. 250–51. Used by permission. The entire chapter is worth reading as a careful coverage of this approach.

[26] Ibid., p. 252.

than we do ourselves. When the book is written, it is written, and it either adds to or subtracts from the happiness of God who shares our emotions as well as our thoughts and values.

To continue to live in God's memory is a view that affords satisfaction to many, for it is a position that commends itself in terms of our knowledge of life and death as well as in terms of what process theology says about the all-encompassing love of a God who enters into our lives. But it does not completely satisfy those who desire to keep some of the old beliefs and hope they can do so on this basis. Norman Pittenger asks plaintively: If God can remember all that we do and are, is this really possible "unless he also values and preserves, keeps and remembers, enjoys and uses us through whom these goods have been achieved?"[27] And Hartshorne's answer to this question, from this perspective, must be no, for one of the limits of our creation and creativity is that it has an end. As Hartshorne writes: "To live everlastingly, as God does, can scarcely be our privilege; but we may earn everlasting places as lives well lived within the one life that not only evermore will have been lived, but evermore and inexhaustively will be lived in ever new ways."[28]

CONCLUSION

Perhaps there is no conclusion to this kind of argument. What has been done in this chapter is to present the great variety of claims as to what happens after death. Not only are there more people who disbelieve in the afterlife, but there are more who are questioning it, and still there are a large number who will be able to choose from the various options. Each person brings to the question of life after death his own presuppositions, ways of thinking, wishes, and desires. Some of them are governed by the fear of death, some by a kind of sweet or sour resignation, some by an

---

[27] W. Norman Pittenger, *Trying to Be a Christian* (Philadelphia: Pilgrim Press, 1972), p. 108.
[28] Hartshorne, *The Logic of Perfection*, p. 262.

acceptance of death as a limit. So each person is free to come to his own conclusions. Perhaps he agrees with Henry Nelson Wieman that death serves God's purposes so well that any other conclusion becomes sacrilege. Or one may be sufficiently impressed by the evidence from psychical research to be convinced that people not only survive death but make return appearances and communicate with survivors who are duly sensitive. Or one may be convinced that there is a soul that can exist without a body and yet be identified, so that there can be a reunion with those we love in an ethereal state. This may lead to an insistence on the Greek idea of immortality, or the Hindu idea of the transmigration of souls, or immortality modified by Christian insights. At this point others may opt for a kind of social immortality, such as found in the Wisdom of Sirach, which stresses continued influence. But those exposed to the teachings of Paul may prefer his insistence on resurrection of a spiritual body, followed by a general resurrection after a period of being asleep, or they may modify this in the direction of immediately being taken into the presence of God as an identifiable personalized spirit. Or there may be an emphasis on the quality of eternal life as something experienced now, which points to the eternal significance of this moment, no matter what may happen later.

The only option which may be new to the reader is that all that we stand for, what we really are in terms of our values and our dreams, our achievements and our hopes, our failures and our faith, may be taken up into God's memory, for he is one who lives from everlasting to everlasting.

This kind of presentation leaves completely open whether we do in any sense survive death. As I get older, I find it harder and harder to conceive of any kind of life after death, except possibly along the lines of Hartshorne's suggestion, and I find that it does not bother me. This may be why I could write the opening chapters of this book without being upset. Death does not seem to me to be a fearful thing to be dreaded, although I have misgivings about the process of dying if it includes too much unnecessary suffering. That is why my wife and I have signed "living wills" to protect ourselves from overenthusiastic heroics when we are on our deathbeds, why I like the idea of the hospice, and why I want my body to be used for medical research.

But I have what I once called "intimations of immortality." There are moments in the lives of most human beings when they sense what we call "eternity." This may be what the Fourth Gospel means by eternal life in the present. There are experiences of groups who come together for common worship and are uplifted by a power they cannot see. There are experiences of listening to truly great music and of feeling that one is looking into the heart of the Eternal. There are ethical actions which are once and for all final, whether it be the sacrifice of a martyr or a hero giving his life to save a child. There is a conviction of "for this cause was I born," and in an instant the entire pattern of one's life is changed. A mother sometimes feels this in the birth of a child; it may come to one who has suffered, and through the patience and witness of that suffering brings others to heroic action or Christian faith; it comes in times of crisis to many men and women, when there are floods, earthquakes, pestilence, and wars which call for sacrifice and service. It can come to all human beings who through their commitment keep themselves sensitive to what they believe to be God's will in every situation, who are flexible enough to change their plans and hopes and desires whenever they see that God's will can be served in a new way, and who see that, though all that is precious may be destroyed, including life itself, there is still God and salvation lies in trust in him. We fulfill God's conditions as best we can, and he provides the growth, the creative transformation, the healing power, and the radiance that makes the Christian way the abundant life. We are comrades of Jesus Christ, heirs of God, and joint heirs with Christ, through whom we find the abundant life. All that we are continues to be meaningful in the memory of God.[29]

---

[29] See Miller, *What We Can Believe,* pp. 196–98.

CHAPTER TEN

Life at
the Limit

The title of this chapter is taken from a book by Graham
Hill, the great racing driver, who called his story *Life
at the Limit*.[1] The racing driver is one who drives a car to
the limit at which his car can just keep its adhesion on the
road in a curve at high speed, who runs the engine at the
utmost speed consistent with holding the motor together,
who pushes himself to the limit of his courage and endur-
ance in order to meet the competition offered by his col-
leagues. There is a great element of risk in auto racing, so
much so that some people think it is an expression of a death
wish. But the drivers do not believe this; they think of taking such risks because of the great mental, spiritual, and
physical satisfaction that comes from such a sport. For them
it is a way of conquering the fear of death, of injury, of
defeat in life.

This recognition that human life has a limit is essential to
mastering the art of dying. No one knows at what point
death will arrive; it may be as an avenging angel, as a delayed visitor who comes long after one is ready, as an early
arrival claiming one's life long before payment is due. There
is a sense in which we may be prepared to die, if we under-

---

[1] Graham Hill, *Life at the Limit* (London: William Kimber, 1969).

stand something of the reasons for it; but in another sense we are not ready when we enter the process of dying and death occurs.

One way in which we can be helped is through death education. Jeremy Taylor wrote: "He who would die well must always look for death, every day knocking on the gates of the grave; and then the gates of the grave can never prevail against him to do him mischief."[2] If this seems to be an overstatement from an age of piety, as I think it is, it still carries with it a kernel of truth: we can come to terms with dying and death only if we understand it sufficiently so that we overcome our fear of it; but most of the time we should forget about it, for those who dwell on the topic and approach it with attitudes of depression, despair, or hopelessness are not free to live creatively. Hope, involvement with other people, and activity stop deterioration and lead to better health.

My own outline for a course in death education would consist of the topics considered in this book. The facts about death should be understood; we should know what it means to die with dignity; we should make plans about our family's future and plan for our own death; we should understand what it means to develop the art of dying so that we have hope. Maybe we need to develop a sense of humor, so that we can say, "Dying is the last thing I will *ever* do!"

LIVE WHILE YOU'RE LIVING

We sometimes hear it said that someone is dead while he is still physically alive. This is obvious when someone is in a coma, but it also applies to those who have stopped living meaningfully even though they are very much alive physically. There are people who are so cautious about protecting their health that they lose all sense of living life at the limit; they withdraw from all risks that give zest and flavor to life, to seek the supposed safety of an utterly bland diet of expe-

---

[2] Jeremy Taylor, *The Rule and Exercise of Holy Dying* (Cleveland: World, 1952), p. 55.

riences that do not contribute to their growth. Our culture sometimes insists that the elderly withdraw from the mainstream of life, and they are literally put on the shelf where they no longer experience being needed within the framework of interpersonal relations; but this experience can also happen to the young in other ways.

Preparation for death, we have said, should take only a little time. It is not healthy to meditate on death much of the time, but it is important to develop a realistic view of death. Most of our time, and it is a limited time for all of us, should be focused on the meaning of living and on living meaningfully. First of all, it is evident that when one sees the meaning of life one can see the meaning of death. "It is only apparently paradoxical that those in love with life are less afraid of death than those who live superficially,"[3] for if we cannot give meaning to life our death also will be meaningless, and this is where the horror comes in. Those who are willing to make a deal with the devil in order to attain a few more years of life find that the additional years have no meaning.[4]

Second, the concept of limit as applied to life sharpens our sense of values. After the death of someone we love we often condemn ourselves for not having enjoyed the opportunities for friendship, for interpersonal relationships, for congenial activities together until it is too late; or we regret that we have acted thoughtlessly, indifferently, or selfishly because we believed we could make it up to that person later, and now he is dead. Certainly the teachings of Jesus against the background of the imminent coming of the kingdom of God sharpen the ethics in the Gospels. "Repent; for the kingdom of Heaven is upon you (Matt. 4:17, NEB)." Paul's saying has the same emphasis: "It is time for you to wake out of sleep, for deliverance is nearer to us now than it was when first we believed. It is far on in the night; day is near (Rom. 13:11–12, NEB)." Because we love life and because we are going to die, we who have a limited time to

---

[3] Ignace Lepp, *Death and Its Mysteries* (New York: Macmillan, 1968), p. 53.
[4] Ibid., p. 149.

live want to avoid alienating other people, for our ethical sensitivity has been sharpened by the realization of death as closing our chances on earth. If we could live forever on earth without death, we would have an everlasting time to correct our mistakes and this would make us even more careless.

Third, we begin to realize that "the tragedy or the victory of death is in the way one dies, not in the fact of death itself."[5] Cabot and Dicks recount the story of a woman who, according to their interpretation, faced death with religious faith. Her chances of surviving an operation were slight, and there was tension in the operating room as she was wheeled in. She asked the chaplain if it would be all right and he had reassured her. Whereupon she said, "Yes, it's all right; whether I get well or whether I die it is all right." She did not die, but her attitude was to the chaplain "religion expressed in its purest form. To attain it is the final triumph of religion."[6]

Robert Browning expressed this attitude in his poem "Prospice":

> Fear death?—to feel the fog in my throat,
>   The mist in my eyes,
> When the snows begin, and the blasts denote
>   I am nearing the place,
> The power of the night, the press of the storm,
>   The post of the foe;
> Where he stands, the Arch Fear in a visible form,
>   Yet the strong man must go:
> For the journey is done and the summit attained,
>   And the barriers fall,
> Though a battle's to fight ere the guerdon be gained,
>   The reward of it all.
> I was ever a fighter, so—one fight more,
>   The best and the last!

---

[5] Richard C. Cabot and Russell L. Dicks, *The Art of Ministering to the Sick* (New York: Macmillan, 1936), p. 314. Used by permission.
[6] Ibid., pp. 299–300.

I would hate that death bandaged my eyes, and forebore,
    And bade me creep past.
No! let me taste the whole of it, fare like my peers
    The heroes of old,
Bear the brunt, in a minute pay glad life's arrears
    Of pain, darkness and cold.
For sudden the worst turns the best to the brave,
    The black minute's at end,
And the element's rage, the fiend-voices that rave,
    Shall dwindle, shall blend,
Shall change, shall become first a peace, out of pain,
    Then a light, then thy breast,
O thou soul of my soul! I shall clasp thee again,
    And with God be the rest![7]

THE MEANING OF LIFE

This is not the place to spell out the meaning of life, the basis of faith, or even a simple doctrine for believers. But we do need to understand that the meaning of death can only be approached by already having worked out the meaning of life, especially your meaning for your life. We have heard it said that there is no real meaning in the ongoing processes and that we as human beings impose our own meanings on what is meaningless by arbitrary decisions. But this is an act of desperation rather than a way of becoming adjusted to reality.

Others say that our convictions need to reflect the meanings found in our existence in this life. The assumption is that in spite of all the absurdity, inequality, suffering, and failures in this world, life offers us meanings which we can appropriate. That this is sometimes difficult we have to admit, for there are situations of early death, unjust treatment, undeveloped potential that make it difficult to see the meaning in every human life. Some lives are cut short or

---

[7] *The Poems and Plays of Robert Browning,* introduction by Saxe Commins (New York: Modern Library, 1934), p. 318.

wasted. Perhaps only God can see the meaning in some human endeavors.

For many the crux of the matter lies in human beings' freedom. Only as we can make choices with some degree of freedom can we find the values that are available in life. We can decide for or against life, for or against certain values, for or against God. We can begin to gain a view of the nature of things in which there are processes working for man's good, and we can begin to measure what we believe to be truth against the reality in which we live. We may not become philosophers, but we begin to think like one.

This leads to the problems of faith and the question of whether we can put our trust in anything at all: in our family, in other human beings, in our culture, in God. Faith as trust is also openness to experience, openness to new insights, openness to the creative good that is beyond our imaginations, and therefore it carries us to new horizons of insight into the meaning of life, and it carries us to the realization that we are caught up in the love of God.[8] At this point the biblical use of the word grace may become meaningful as we realize that God acts to bring us within the scope of his love through reconciliation with him and our fellow human beings.

Paul Tillich has expressed this in a different vocabulary:

It is as though a voice were saying: "You are accepted. *You are accepted,* accepted by that which is greater than you, and the name of which you do not know. Do not ask for the name now; perhaps you will find it later. Do not try to do anything now; perhaps later you will do much. Do not seek for anything; do not perform anything; do not intend anything. *Simply accept the fact that you are accepted!"* If that happens to us, we experience grace. After such an experience we may not be better than before, and we may not believe more than before. But everything is transformed. In that moment, grace conquers sin, and recon-

[8] See Bernard E. Meland, *Faith and Culture* (London: George Allen & Unwin, 1955), p. 119; Schubert M. Ogden, *The Reality of God* (New York: Harper & Row, 1966), p. 220.

ciliation bridges the gulf of estrangement. And nothing is demanded of this experience, no religious or moral or intellectual presupposition, nothing but *acceptance*.[9]

For many of us, building on the quotation from Tillich or from a similar or parallel experience, this leads to belief in God. We believe that just because we are defeated, God is not defeated. Because God works through the processes of creativity and growth, we believe that when God is hindered in one direction his work springs up in another one. His work is not destroyed, even though on a particular patch of earth his work finds rocks or shallow ground rather than rich soil.

As long as there is God, there is a basis for human hope. As Christians we worship the God of Jesus Christ, with the promise that we can be transformed by being renewed in our total persons, can be reconciled with other human beings, and can find meaning in this life when we seek to be in the right relation with him. This is the point at which life becomes meaningful for many people. Dag Hammarskjöld wrote: "But at some moment I did answer *Yes* to Someone —or Something—and from that hour I was certain that existence is meaningful and that, therefore, my life, in self-surrender, had a goal."[10]

After having had a heart attack, the psychologist Abraham Maslow spoke of his "post-mortem life." He wrote:

My attitude toward life changed. The word I use for it now is the post-mortem life. I could just as easily have died so that my living constitutes a kind of an extra, a bonus. It's all gravy. Therefore I might just as well live as if I had already died.

One very important aspect of the post-mortem life is that everything gets doubly precious, gets piercingly important. You get stabbed by things, by flowers and by babies and by beautiful

[9] Paul Tillich, *The Shaking of the Foundations* (New York: Charles Scribner's Sons, 1948), p. 162. Used by permission.
[10] From *Markings*, by Dag Hammarskjöld, p. xii. Copyright © 1964 by Alfred A. Knopf, Inc. and Faber & Faber, Ltd. Reprinted by permission of the publishers.

things—just the very act of living, of walking and breathing and eating and having friends and chatting. Everything seems to look more beautiful rather than less, and one gets the much-intensified sense of miracles. . . .

If you're reconciled with death or even if you are pretty well assured that you will have a good death, a dignified one, then every single moment of every single day is transformed because the pervasive undercurrent—the fear of death—is removed. . . . I am living an end-life where everything ought to be an end in itself, where I shouldn't be wasting time preparing for the future, or occupying myself with means to later ends.[11]

Will Rogers once wrote that no religious revival will ever come from arguments over where we came from but over where we are going. He added:

When I die, my epitaph or whatever you call those signs on gravestones is going to read: "I joked about every prominent man of my time, but I never met a man I didn't like." I am so proud of that I can hardly wait to die so it can be carved. And when you come to see my grave you will find me sitting there, proudly reading it.[12]

Whimsy and humor are combined with a serious faith in the meaning of life.

Emerson W. Harris has written a brief poem which expresses another side of belief from that of Will Rogers:

> I heard a good man say
> At the funeral of a friend
> That unless he believed in immortality of the soul
> There was nothing to live for,

---

[11] Excerpted from the August 1970 editorial in *Psychology Today* magazine. Copyright © Communications/Research/Machines, Inc.; cited in Donald P. Irish, *Death Education*, ed. Betty R. Green and Donald P. Irish (Cambridge, Mass.: Schenkman, 1971), p. 46.

[12] From *The Will Rogers Book*, compiled by Paula McSpadden Love (Waco, Tex.: Texian Press, 1961), pp. 166–67. Used by permission.

Nothing to hope for;
It was the hope of immortality that gave his life
What of meaning and richness he knew he had found.
I could not agree with him.
The way I see it:
Immortality is like a maraschino cherry
On a strawberry shortcake.
The cherry adds color
And taste to the delicacy,
But if it were not there,
I would find the cake and the berries
And the whipped cream to be quite delicious.
And this would be sufficient, and I would say,
"God, thanks for the strawberries and the cake and
The whipped cream.
Put the cherry on if you wish,
But without the cherry the rest is enough.
Thanks, God, for life."[13]

We cannot tell you what the meaning of life is for you, but we can say that unless you can find meaning in the world around you, you won't find much meaning in death, but if you do discover a meaningful attitude toward life you can find meaning in death as well.

EARLY DEATH

That we die becomes a necessity, and it is possible to enter the process of dying and to accept death with a healthy attitude and religious faith. The problem becomes acute when we consider the timing of death, for premature death compounds the question of dying. Yet there are various kinds of premature death and we react in different ways to its occurrence.

There is a premature death that is voluntary: the hero who takes great risks to save someone else and as a result

[13] "Strawberry Shortcake," *The Churchman,* Oct. 1971, p. 9. Used by permission.

loses his or her life. We regret his death, but we can see the reason for it. The martyr who risks his life because he stands for something or acts against injustice and is put to death because of it is admired even when the reaction is grief; this accounts for the response of the nation to the assassinations of John Kennedy and Martin Luther King, as well as to the many "lesser" martyrs who for political or moral reasons have been killed on college campuses and elsewhere. Sometimes these deaths are shocking because we intuit the moral value expressed in their lives so far. Jonathan Edwards, who was the president of Princeton University, died because he set an example by being vaccinated for smallpox. There have been many scientists and other volunteers who have risked death in experiments that have benefited mankind. So we have a roll call of heroes and martyrs whose deaths have been voluntary (at least to the extent of taking great risks) in the service of truth or of God or of fellow human beings.

But there are many other kinds of premature deaths that shake our confidence in life or our faith in God. In spite of modern achievements in science, in human competence, in medicine, in transportation, there are accidents. People are killed in industrial accidents, coal mines, airplanes, automobiles, motorcycles, and walking down the street. Children on bicycles or sleds still get run over. There are great natural calamities such as earthquakes, tornadoes, fires, volcanoes, and tidal waves which kill people wholesale. The elements kill people, as they are isolated and die from hunger, thirst, and exposure. People freeze to death. Swimming is dangerous in shark-infested waters; animals still kill people.

However, the most shocking premature deaths are still the kinds executed by human beings on others. War does not kill as many people as automobiles do, but the purpose is different. Even saturation bombing, with its impersonality of radar-focused targets, is still death imposed by human beings on other human beings, and dying wholesale is still individualized and personal for those who die. Violent death due to murder in all its variations of manslaughter or accident with malice fits into the same category. Many people still favor death by execution for those who take the lives of others, which leads to other premature deaths.

A particularly poignant kind of premature death is that which occurs while physical life continues. The most obvious instance is that of insanity leading to loss of identity, but it may exist at various levels where commitment to an institution for life is the result. Another form of this is senility, which may be a protection in some cases but is also a way of losing identity while remaining physically alive. By stretching a point, we can point to the oppressed who never have an opportunity to live meaningfully, who are physically alive at the borderline of nutrition and health and find few if any satisfactions in life.

Chiefly, however, the premature death that bothers most of us is that of being struck down by illness and dying at an early age.[14] There are killing diseases that strike children and young adults. What we see is the wiping out of potentialities for the values that might be given to the world, the cutting off of life in its prime, the termination of vocations such as motherhood or fatherhood. It is hard to reconcile such premature deaths with any positive attitude toward death.

What can we make of premature death? Is there a possible religious answer to the question? Can we maintain faith in a God of love in the light of sudden death? I believe that there are ways of thinking about God and the world which may help us.

In the litany, one form of prayer used in many churches, there is this petition:

From lightning and tempest; from earthquake, fire, and flood; from plague, pestilence, and famine; from battle and murder, and from sudden death,
  Good Lord, deliver us.

---

[14] See John B. Coburn, *Anne and the Sand Dobbies* (New York: Seabury Press, 1964); John Gunther, *Death, Be Not Proud* (New York: Harper & Row, 1949).

Here is a recognition of the problem. It asks God to free us from premature death, and yet there is little change except in the area of infant mortality. People keep on dying long before they or we think they should.

How can we relate this to the belief in a God of love? I once tried to work this out against the background of a premature death, and I began with the assertion that "God is love, and he who abides in love abides in God, and God abides in him (1 John 4:16b, RSV)." If we analyze the meaning of the word love we end up by believing that love must be dependable, and this constancy of God's love is crucial for our faith in him. Yet the dependableness of this love in facing premature death is what hurts us.

Science has made clear what Christianity used to talk about: natural law. Our relation to our world is based on the assumption that it is dependable and consistent, whether we are in a scientific laboratory or on the highway. While no one ever sees a natural law, we do observe the consistency of events, and this is what gives us confidence in our knowledge, our expectations, and our predictions of the future. It is why we know that death is inevitable.

We are willing to live with the consequences of natural law, which is strikingly impartial. When the winds blow and the floods come, we need to do the adapting if we are to survive. When a virus strikes down a young mother we are helpless unless medical science has discovered a cure. When there is an epidemic that kills thousands, we observe the wholesale tragedy but can do nothing to change the situation. What we see is a *combination* of natural factors that lead to evil, which is not the result of any single natural law in itself.

Premature death is often due to such a combination of natural laws. I do not believe that God *wills* such deaths, a belief that causes such distress among the uncritically pious. Because God is dependable in his goodness and his love, he is not going to reverse the natural law through which he works as the creative good. In a world in which freedom and chance exist under the providence of a God of love, we look on such deaths as unpredictable, yet we can discover the causes of such deaths. But from the point of view of those who could not predict such deaths, they appear to be due to chance. No one could predict that the virus and the person would meet at a certain place and at a time when the person was susceptible, just as no one could predict that an airplane would fall when that person was traveling on it.

I do not see that such an interpretation is inconsistent with an understanding of a loving God. There are elements of freedom and chance even in the dependableness of the natural world, in that man cannot predict exactly when and where something will happen, and this applies especially to death. We do not see reversals of natural law, however. No matter how one interprets the resurrection, it is a fact that Jesus did not escape from the cross and he died as a common criminal executed by a Roman government. But we may believe that God shared in the suffering of the cross, as he shares in the suffering of all human beings.

A statement by D. R. Davies has helped me to see the power of God's love in the face of man's freedom, suffering, and death. He wrote:

What is love? Love is the power to grant freedom without desiring to limit or inhibit its exercise. It is the power to give freedom without any will to take it back. *And it is only omnipotence that can refrain absolutely from trespassing upon freedom.* Only God can give and not take back. In all human history and experience, without exception, the supreme thing which man cannot do is to permit the untrammeled exercise of the power of self-determination. But God not only permits it. He encourages it. He suffers in Himself the entire consequence of allowing man absolute freedom. That is His love. It is also His omnipotence, which may be defined as the will and capacity to endure everything that man may inflict upon God through the exercise of freedom. And that takes some doing![15]

---

[15] D. R. Davies, *Down Peacock's Feathers* (New York: Macmillan, 1944), p. 23. Used by permission.

"There is no fear in love, but perfect love casts out fear (1 John 4:18a, RSV)." This is the great victory of a mature faith. It is never completely achieved, because we cannot maintain a consistent relation to God's perfect love. Our certainty of God's love is the basis for our lack of fear in the face of death, premature or in the fulfillment of life, and in the face of the death of those whom we love.

Men face the loss of their wives and wives of their husbands at an early age. In Ezekiel we read: "So I spoke to the people in the morning, and at evening my wife died (Ezek. 24:1a, RSV)." Arthur Gossip preached a sermon after his wife died on the topic "But When Life Tumbles In, What Then?"[16] It is, he says, a test of one's faith, and in the testing faith is strengthened. Scripture passages that have seemed dead spring to life as forms of strength and reassurance.

Like as a father pitieth his children, mused a psalmist long ago. I have been wondering these days whether he, too, poor soul, had suddenly, without one second's warning, to tell his children that their mother was dead, and that remembrance of that agony made him sure all his days it is not willingly that God afflicts and grieves us children of men. Anyhow that is true.[17]

For Gossip, also, his wife's death led him to an assurance that there is immortality and that death itself cannot separate us from the love of God.

Sudden death is always a possibility, and some can say that "whether I live or die, it is all right." One person faced an operation and as she approached the operating theater she sang to herself the hymn of Saint Patrick:

> Christ be with me, Christ within me,
> Christ behind me, Christ before me,

[16] "But When Life Tumbles In, What Then?," *Protestant Sermons,* ed. Andrew W. Blackwood (Nashville: Abington Press, 1947), pp. 198–204; from *The Hero in Thy Soul* (New York: Charles Scribner's Sons, 1929). Used by permission.

[17] Ibid., p. 202.

Christ beside me, Christ to win me. . . .
I bind unto myself the Name,
The strong Name of the Trinity.[18]

Finally, when death is approaching and the end is irrevo-
cable, there are the reassuring words of the psalmist:

> I will lift up mine eyes unto the hills; from whence cometh
> my help?
> My help cometh even from the Lord, who hath made
> heaven and earth.
> He will not suffer thy foot to be moved; and he that keep-
> eth thee will not sleep.
> Behold, he that keepeth Israel shall neither slumber nor
> sleep.
> The Lord himself is thy keeper; the Lord is thy defence
> upon thy right hand;
> So that the sun shall not burn thee by day, neither the
> moon by night.
> The Lord shall preserve thee from all evil; yea, it is even
> he that shall keep thy soul.
> The Lord shall preserve thy going out, and thy coming in,
> from this time forth for evermore.[19]

—Psalm 121, PB

LONG LIVE GOD!

"It is a hard lesson to learn—that God is more important
than we are."[20] God is deeply involved in our living and
dying, and his own nature is qualified by what happens to
his creatures. His love is constant and consistent, but because
he is love he can take our thoughts and feelings and values

---

[18] *The Hymnal 1940*, no. 268, stanzas 6 and 7.
[19] See R. C. Miller, *Living with Anxiety* (Philadelphia: Pilgrim Press, 1971),
pp. 157–62, for an approach similar to that of this section.
[20] Charles Hartshorne and William L. Reese, eds., *Philosophers Speak of
God* (Chicago: University of Chicago Press, 1953), p. 285; see also Daniel
Day Williams, *God's Grace and Man's Hope* (New York: Harper & Row,
1949), pp. 56–57.

upon himself or into himself, and this means that he can change even if his love does not. Many people who are unable to form any kind of view of God or the hereafter are aware of a divine presence as they face dying and death.

The emphasis is on God, and yet it is our dying that we are concerned with. This is the proper balance, for I cannot get away from my own living and dying, and yet I am free to face both life and death only as I see my life grounded in those creative and meaningful processes which support and strengthen the meaning of my own life. If I am fortunate, my life has a degree of fulfillment before it is brought to a close. We can offer both our living and our dying as a gift, a sacrifice, to a loving God.

The story of Simeon, an old man who took the infant Jesus in his arms and then was fulfilled and ready to die, clarifies this approach to dying:

> Now let your servant, Almighty Master,
> Slip away quietly in peace, as you've said.
> For these eyes of mine have seen your deliverance
> Which you have made possible for *all* of the people.
> It's a light to illuminate the problem of races,
> A light to bring honor to your faithful disciples.[21]

Simeon illustrates what we have meant by the art of dying. He waited until the fulfillment of seeing the Messiah, and he saw that this meant the possibility of new relations between races and a new light to *all* people. Then he could die in peace, for he had captured the meaning his life was waiting for. He knew what it meant to "live until you die."

At the conclusion of the musical *Godspell*, after Jesus has been crucified, there is a repeated refrain that expresses the meaning of living and dying. The cry is "Long live God! Long live God!" Perhaps this is the end of the matter, and it is what makes the art of dying in relation to a living and loving God meaningful: "Long live God!" Amen.

---

[21] Clarence Jordan, *The Cotton Patch Version of Luke and Acts*, Luke 2:29–32 (New York: Association Press, 1969), p. 20.

For More Information

For those who want more information, there are a number of books. I have listed first the easy-to-read books that deal with death as such, then a few books that deal with the future, followed by some of the technically written books that I found indispensable, and finally a few books for children.

A survey of the research in the field, with a development of the denial-acceptance view of death, is found in *The American View of Death: Acceptance or Denial?* by Richard G. Dumont and Dennis C. Foss (Cambridge, Mass.: Schenkman Publishing Co. and General Learning Press, 1972). In simple and reliable fashion this book gives an interesting overall view.

The most interesting book on the subject, because it presents a number of interviews with terminally ill patients and provides a basis for seminars on death education, is *On Death and Dying,* by Elisabeth Kübler-Ross (New York: Macmillan, 1969). She presents an outline of the stages that those expecting to die go through and shows how a psychiatrist or clergyman or family can be of help. But the chief information comes from the terminal patients.

There have been some symposia on death recently, and one of the most helpful is summarized in *Death Education: Preparation for Living,* edited by Betty R. Green and Donald P. Irish (Cambridge, Mass.: Schenkman Publishing Co. and General Learning Press, 1971). Among the contributors are Herman Feifel, John P. Brantner, Daniel Leviton, and Donald Irish. The emphasis is on the need for death education in the schools, and there is a discussion following the position papers on how various groups are involved in death education as learners and teachers.

One of the most fascinating reports is in *Death and Presence,* edited by André Godin (Brussels: Lumen Vitae Press, 1972). He brings together information, mostly from Europe, based on research into attitudes toward death and the afterlife, with reports from outstanding researchers. It reflects the revolution in current thinking about death.

For those who want to test their attitudes concerning death, the series of exercises in *The Art of Dying* by Robert E. Neale (New York: Harper & Row, 1973) will be both stimulating and helpful.

A history of Christian thinking about death and resurrection from early times until today will be found in *Death: Meaning and Morality in Christian Thought and Contemporary Culture* by Milton McC. Gatch (New York: Seabury Press, 1969).

The Modern Vision of Death, edited by Nathan A. Scott, Jr. (Richmond: John Knox Press, 1967), includes a variety of approaches in literature, philosophy, and science, and a fascinating account of "The Time My Father Died," by Joseph W. Mathews. Amos N. Wilder, J. Glenn Gray, Hans J. Morgenthau, Joseph Haroutunian, and Paul Tillich are the other contributors.

A psychological approach that deals with both death and the afterlife is *Death and Its Mysteries,* by Ignace Lepp (New York: Macmillan, 1968). He stresses the fact that only as we find meaning in life can we find it in death, and he builds his view of an afterlife on the philosophy of Teilhard de Chardin.

There is concern about the future. A particularly helpful book is *Hope and the Future of Man*, edited by Ewert H. Cousins (Philadelphia: Fortress Press, 1972). It is the report of a conference involving well-known theologians, including John B. Cobb, Jr., Jürgen Moltmann, Wolfhart Pannenberg, and others. There is a variety of viewpoints.

Four Ingersoll Lectures on Immortality are reprinted in *Immortality and Resurrection*, edited by Krister Stendahl (New York: Macmillan, 1965). Oscar Cullmann provides a controversial interpretation of the New Testament view of resurrection, and Henry J. Cadbury indicates Jesus' interpretation of immortality. The Greeks and the church fathers are interpreted by Harry A. Wolfson and Werner Jaeger.

"Time, Death, and Everlasting Life," an essay on what it means to have one's "book of life" continued in the memory of God, is found on pages 245–62 of *The Logic of Perfection* by Charles Hartshorne (LaSalle, Ill.: Open Court Publishing Co., 1962). This may well be the most significant treatment of "life" after death by a process theologian.

In 1959, Herman Feifel edited what may have been the breakthrough book on *The Meaning of Death* (New York: McGraw-Hill, 1959). Eighteen chapters, all technical, deal with theoretical outlooks, views of children, cultural outlooks, and experimental data, all of which were significant.

Another book, very much like Feifel's in some ways, *Death and Identity*, edited by Robert Fulton (New York: John Wiley & Sons, 1965), consists of reports of careful studies of various aspects of death and grief, as seen by different groups in our society, such as children, mentally ill patients, and the elderly.

Avery D. Weisman, in *On Dying and Denying* (New York: Behavioral Publications, 1972), sees dying as a dynamic aspect of living, and looks at the psychosocial stages through which a person goes as he moves toward death. There are many brief case studies to illuminate his points.

Many aspects of death are treated in *Man's Concern with Death* (London: Hodder & Stoughton, 1968; New York: McGraw-Hill, 1969), which includes chapters by Arnold

Toynbee, A. Keith Mant, Ninian Smart, John Hinton, Simon Yudkin, Eric Rhode, Rosalind Heywood, and H. H. Price. There is a great variety of topics, mostly on attitudes toward death, as well as two long chapters on psychical research.

A more specifically Christian approach to death is found in *Perspectives on Death*, edited by Liston O. Mills (Nashville: Abingdon Press, 1969). There are chapters on the Old and New Testament views of death, death in the early church and on through the Reformation, death in contemporary literature, and perspectives on death and the care of the dying today.

The care of the dying becomes an important part of our relations with friends and relatives. Most books are for the clergy, but we can learn from them. A small book by Carl G. Carlozzi, *Death and Contemporary Man* (Grand Rapids: Eerdmans, 1968), might prove helpful to lay people. More technical is *Counseling the Dying*, by Margaretta K. Bowers, Edgar N. Jackson, James A. Knight, and Lawrence McShan (New York: Thomas Nelson & Sons, 1964).

There is not much material for small children. Among the best is the material for kindergarten and first grade in the curriculum of the Anglican Church of Canada. Some help can be found in *Explaining Death to Children*, edited by Earl A. Grollman (Boston: Beacon Press, 1967), and in his simple *Talking About Death* (Boston: Beacon Press, 1970), which can be used with children. An important book for children from about nine up and for parents is *Anne and the Sand Dobbies*, by John B. Coburn (New York: Seabury Press, 1964). *My Grandpa Died Today*, by Joan Fassler (New York: Behavioral Publications, 1971), is particularly suitable for children in that situation.

Index

153

About the Author

Randolph Crump Miller, a native of Fresno, California, is a well-known religious educator, pastor, editor of *Religious Education*, and author of numerous books, including *Living with Anxiety, The Language Gap and God, Education for Christian Living, Your Child's Religion, The Clue to Christian Education,* and *Christian Nurture and the Church.*

An ordained clergyman in the Episcopal Church, Dr. Miller has been pastor of local churches in California, a religious education minister, and is now Horace Bushnell Professor of Christian Nurture, Yale Divinity School. He is a graduate of Pomona College and Yale University and lives in New Haven, Connecticut.